Virginia County Records

VOLUME VIII

A Key to

SOUTHERN PEDIGREES

Being a Comprehensive Guide to the Colonial Ancestry of Families in
the States of Virginia, Maryland, Georgia, North Carolina,
South Carolina, Kentucky, Tennessee, West Virginia
and Alabama

EDITED BY

William Armstrong Crozier

CLEARFIELD

Reprinted for
Clearfield Company by
Genealogical Publishing Co.
Baltimore, Maryland
2000, 2001, 2004, 2007

ISBN-13: 978-0-8063-0471-7
ISBN-10: 0-8063-0471-5

Originally published as Volume VIII
of *Virginia County Records*
Hasbrouck Heights, New Jersey, ca. 1910-1911
Reprinted: Southern Book Company
Baltimore, 1953
Reprinted: Genealogical Publishing Co., Inc.
Baltimore, 1971, 1978, 1985
Library of Congress Catalogue Card Number 67-29835

Virginia County Record Publications

VOLUME VIII

A KEY TO

Southern Pedigrees

Being a Comprehensive Guide to the Colonial Ancestry of Families in the States of Virginia, Maryland, Georgia, North Carolina, South Carolina, Kentucky, Tennessee, West Virginia and Alabama

EDITED BY

WILLIAM ARMSTRONG CROZIER, F. R. S., F. G. S. A.

Editor of the Virginia County Records, etc., etc.

THE GENEALOGICAL ASSOCIATION
Publishers
Hasbrouck Heights   New Jersey

Virginia County Records

Abbott. Va. Co. Records I.

Abell. Wood's Hist. of Albemarle, Va.

Abernathy. Chamberlyne's Bristol Par. Reg. The Descendants of John Walker of Wigton, Scot., by Emma S. White, 1902.

Abney. Va. Co. Records I.

Abrahall. Va. Co. Records V.

Ackiss. The Lower Norfolk Co. Antiquary.

Acton. Founders of Anne Arundel and Howard Cos., Md., by Warfield, 1905.

Adams. Va. Hist. Mag., IV, VIII, IX. Wm. and Mary Quar., V, VI, XIII, XIX. Moore's Annals of Henrico Par., Va. St. Peter's Par. Reg., New Kent, Va. Va. Co. Records V, VI. The Woods-McAfee Memorial, by Woods and Durett, 1905. Hist. of Bulloch Families, by Joseph G. Bulloch, 1892.

Addison. St. Peter's Par. Reg., New Kent, Va. Chamberlyne's Bristol Par. Reg.

Aitcheson. Wm. and Mary Quar., XIII. Va. Co. Rec., V.

Alexander. Foote's Sketches of Va., II. Hayden's Va. Gen. Richmond Standard, I, II, III. Johnston's Old Va. Clerks. Wm. and Mary Quar., II, V, VI, VII, VIII, IX, X, XI. Va. Mag., X. Va. Co. Records, II, V. The Peden Family of So. Car., by Hewell, 1900. The Woods-McAfee Memorial, by Woods and Durett, 1905. Records of the Alexander Fam., by F. A. Butterworth, 1909.

Alden. Middlesex Par. Reg., Va.

Alford. St. Peter's Par. Reg., Va.

Alfriend. Robertson's Pocahontas' Descendants, 1887.

Allan. Va. Co. Records, I, II.

Allen. Hayden's Va. Gen. Wm. and Mary Quar., VI, VII, VIII. Va. Co. Records, I, II, V, VI. Middlesex Par. Reg., Va. St. Peter's Par. Reg., Va. Clarke's Old King William, Va. Homes and Fam. Chamberlyne's Bristol Par. Reg., Va. Habersham Hist. Coll. Ga., I. Green's Kentucky Families, 1889.

Allerton. Va. Mag., I. New Eng. Hist. Reg., Vol. 44. Wm. and Mary Quar., IV, XVII. Lee of Va., by L. J. Lee, 1895. Of Sceptred Race, by Watson, 1910. Notable Fam. of America, by Watson, 1898. Allerton of New Eng. and Va., by Greenwood, 1890. The Allerton Fam. in the U. S., by W. S. Allerton, 1888.

Alley. Chamberlyne's Bristol Par. Reg. Va.

Alphin. Wood's Hist. of Albemarle, Va.

Alsobrook. Richmond, Va., Standard, IV.

Alsop. Va. County Records, I.

Alston. The Alstons of No. and So. Carolina, by J. A. Groves, 1902. So. Car. Hist. Mag., 1906.

Ambler. Meade's Old Fam. and Churches of Va., I. Richmond, Va., Standard, I, III. McIlhany's Some Va. Families, 1903. Coll. of Va. Hist. Society, V. Goodwyn's Hist. of Bruton Church, Va. Wm. and Mary Quar., V, XIII. Tyler's Cradle of the Republic, 1906. Va. County Records, V. Richmond, Va., Critic, 20th Jan., 1889.

Ames. Wm. and Mary Quar., XVIII.

Ammonet. Habersham, Ga. Hist. Coll., Vol. II. Coll. of Va. Hist. Soc., V.

Anderson. Richmond, Va., Standard, II, III. Munsell's American Ancestry, VII. Wm. and Mary Quar., IV, XI, XII, XIV. Boogher's Gleanings of Va. History, 1903. The Thomas Book, 1896. Wood's Hist. of Albemarle. Va. Co. Records, I, VI, VII. Chamberlyne's Bristol Par. Reg., 1898. Middlesex Par. Reg. Va. Goodwyn's Bruton Church, Va. Crawford Fam. of Va. Anderson's Robertson Genealogy, 1900. The Anderson Fam., by Thomas McArthur Anderson, N. P. N. D. MSS. Pedigree of the Genealogical Assn., Hasbrouck Heights, N. J.

Andrews. Va. Hist. Mag., II. Wm. and Mary Quar., III, IV, V, VI. Chamberlyne's Bristol Par. Reg., 1898. Va. Co. Records, V, VI, VII. The Thomas Book, 1896. The Maryland Andrews Fam., by Robert Andrews, 1893.

Anthony. Va. Hist. Mag., IX.

Apperson. Va. Co. Records, I. St. Peter's Par. Reg., New Kent, Va. Wm. and Mary Quar., VIII.

Appleton. Wm. and Mary Quar., IV.

Applewhaite. Wm. and Mary Quar., VII.

Archer. Meade's Old Fam. and Churches, I. Richmond, Va., Critic, 1888. Richmond, Va., Standard, III. Robertson's Pocahontas' Desc., 1887. Chamberlyne's Bristol Par. Reg., 1898. Va. Co. Records, V, VI.

Ariss. Crozier's Hist. of Buckner Fam. of Va., 1907. Va. Hist. Mag., IV. Wm. and Mary Quar., XVII.

Armistead. Oliver's Carter Fam. Tree, 1897. Hayden's Va. Gen. Keith's Harrison Ancestry. Richmond, Va., Standard, II, III. Slaughter's Hist. of St. Mark's Par., Va. Paxton's Marshall Gen. Wm. and Mary Quar., VI, VII, VIII, IX, XI, XII, XIV, XVII, XVIII. Va. Hist. Mag., II, III, V, X, XI. Coll. of Va. Hist. Soc., V. Goodwyn's Hist. of Bruton Church. Va. Co. Records, V, VI. Lee of Va., by Edmund J. Lee, 1895. Tyler's Letters of the Tylers, 1897. Appleton's Armistead of Va., 1899. MSS. Ped. of the Genealogical Assn., Hasbrouck Heights, N. J.

Armstrong. Slaughter's Hist. of St. Mark's Par., Va. Gray's McGavock Fam., 1903. Woods-McAfee Memorial, by Woods and Durett, 1905. Va. Co. Records, II.

Arnest. Wm. and Mary Quar., IX.

Arnold. Va. Co. Records, I, II.

Arundel. Va. Hist. Mag., I, II.

Ashby. Hayden's Va. Gen. Green's Hist. of Culpeper Co., Va. Crozier's Hist. of Buckner Fam., 1907. Va. Hist. Mag., VI. Wm. and Mary Quar., XVIII. Va. Co. Records, IV.

Ashley. Va. Co. Records, VI.

Ashmead. Hayden's Va. Gen.

Ashton. Va. Hist. Mag., II, X. Wm. and Mary Quar., IV, VII, VIII. Va. Co. Records, V. Lee of Va., by E. J. Lee. MSS. Ped. of Genealogicl Assn., Hasbrouck Heights, N. J.

Aston. Wm. and Mary Quar., IV. Va. Hist. Mag., III. Va. Co. Records, V.

Atkinson. Slaughter's Hist. of Bristol Par., Va. St. Peter's Par. Reg., Va. Clarke's Old King William Families, 1897. Chamberlyne's Bristol Par. Reg., 1898. Va. Co. Records, V, VI. MSS. Ped. of Genealogical Assn., Hasbrouck Heights, N. J.

Atwood. Middlesex Par. Reg., Va. Lower Norfolk Co. Antiquary, Va.

Austin. St. Peter's Par. Reg., Va. Va. Co. Records, VI.

Axtell. So. Car. Hist. Mag., 1906.

Aylett. Richmond, Va., Standard, II. Slaughter's Hist. of St. Mark's Par., Va. Habersham Hist. Coll. of Ga., I. Va. Hist. Mag., V. Wm. and Mary Quar., V, IX, XV, XVII. Clarke's Old King William Fam., 1897. Lee of Va., by E. J. Lee. Watson's Of Sceptred Race, 1910.

Ayres. Wm. and Mary Quar., VII.

Bacon. Campbell's Hist. of Va. Keith's Harrison Ancestry. Neill's Va. Carolorum. Richmond, Va., Standard, I, II, III. Wm. and Mary Quar., I, II, IV, VII, IX, X, XI. Va. Hist. Mag., II, XIV, XV. New Eng. Hist. and Genl. Reg., XXXVII. St. Peter's Par. Reg., Va. Va. Co. Records, V.

Bagnall. Va. Hist. Mag., VI. Wm. and Mary Quar., VII.

Bagwell. Va. Co. Records, VI. Va. Hist. Mag., V.

Bailey. Slaughter's St. Mark's Par., Va. St. Peter's Par. Reg., Va. Chamberlyne's Bristol Par. Reg., Va., 1898. Habersham Hist. Coll. of Ga., II. Va. County Records, II. VI.

Baillie. Habersham Hist. Coll. of Ga., I, II. Hist. of Bulloch Fam., 1902.

Baker. Va. Hist. Mag., IV. Middlesex, Va., Par. Reg. Wm. and Mary Quar., IV, VI, VII. Va. Co. Records, II, V, VI, VII.

Baldridge. Wm. and Mary Quar., IV, XV.

Baldwin. Hayden's Va. Gen. Peyton's Hist. of Augusta Co., Va. Richmond, Va., Standard, III. Middlesex, Va., Par. Reg. Va. Co. Records, VI, VII. Warfield's Anne Arundel and Howard Cos., Md. Baldwin Gen., by C. C. Baldwin, N. D.

Ball. Pryor's The Mother of Washington. Oliver's Carter Fam. Middlesex Par. Reg., Va. Goode's Va. Cousins, 1887. Hayden's Va. Gen. Meade's Old Churches and Fam., II. Richmond Standard, III. Wm. and Mary Quar., III, IV, V, VI, VIII, XI. Va. Hist. Mag., VII, VIII. Green's Hist. of Culpeper Co., Va. Va. Co. Records, I, II, IV, V. The Maternal Ancestry of Washington, 1885. Ball Family of So. Carolina, by Anne S. Deas, 1909.

Ballance. Munsell's American Ancestry, VII.

Ballard. Neill's Va. Carolorum. Wm. and Mary Quar., I, II, III, V, VII, IX. Va. Hist. Mag., IV, XI. Wood's Hist. of Albemarle Co., Va. Va. Co. Records, I, II, VI, VII. Middlesex, Va., Par. Reg. Goodwyn's Hist. of Bruton Church, Va. MSS. Ped. of the Genealogical Assn.

Ballentine. Wm. and Marv Quar., IV.

Banister. Campbell's Hist. of Va. Richmond, Va., Standard, II.
Slaughter's Hist. of Bristol Par. Va. Hist. Mag., IX, XI. Chamberlyne's Bristol Par. Reg., 1898. Horner's Hist. of the Blair, Banister and Braxton Families, 1898. The Bland Papers.

Bankes. Wm. and Mary Quar., V, VI, VIII.

Bankhead. Hayden's Va. Gen. Wm. and Mary Quar., XIV. Saunder's Early Settlers of Ala., 1899. The Page Family, by R. C. M. Page, 1883.

Banks. Va. Hist. Mag., V. Middlesex Par. Reg. Lower Norfolk Co., Va., Antiquary. Saunder's Early Settlers of Ala., 1899.

Baptist. Neill's Va. Carolorum. Goode's Va. Cousins.

Barber. Goodwyn's Hist of Bruton Church, Va. Wm. and Mary Quar., XVII. Chamberlyne's Bristol Par. Reg., 1898.

Barbour. Slaughter's St. Mark's Par. Green's Hist. of Culpeper Co., Va. Va. Co. Records, I, VI, VII. Scott's Hist. of Orange Co., Va., 1907. Green's Kentucky Families.

Barclay. Wood's Hist. of Albemarle Co., Va. Moffat's Barclay Family, 1904.

Barker. Va. Co. Records, II, VII, VIII.

Barkley. Richmond, Va., Standard, III.

Barksdale. Goode's Va. Cousins. Wood's Hist. of Albemarle Co., Va. Barksdale Fam., by Sarah D. Hubert, 1895.

Barlow. Middlesex Par. Reg., Va. Va. Co. Records, VI, VII.

Barnes. Hayden's Va. Gen. St. Peter's Par. Reg., Va. Lower Norfolk Co. Antiquary.

Barnett. Gilmer's Georgians, 1855. Gibbons-Butcher Gen., by G. B. Gibbens, 1894. St. Peter's Par. Reg., Va.

Barns. Va. Hist. Mag., VII.

Barnwell. Heyward's Barnwell Chart of So. Carolina, 1898. So. Car. Hist. Mag., II.

Barradall. Meade's Old Fam. and Churches, I. Goodwyne's Hist. of Bruton Church, Va. Va. Co. Records, V.

Barrand. Richmond, Va., Standard, II. Hanson's Old Kent, Md.

Barraud. Wm. and Mary Quar., VIII.

Barrett. Va. Hist. Mag., V, VI. Wm. and Mary Quar., VII, IX, Rev. Robert Barrett of Va., and his descendants (chart), compiled by E. A. Claypool, Chicago, 1901.

Barron. Va. Co. Records, VI, VII.

Barry. Habersham Hist. Coll. Ga., I.

Bartlett. Va. Co. Records, I, VI, VII.

Baskerville. Goode's Va. Cousins. Richmond, Va., Standard, III. Va. Hist. Mag., XII, XV. Wm. and Mary Quar., IV, XVII. Va. Co. Records, V.

Baskin. Goode's Va. Cousins.

Bass. Neill's Va. Carolorum. Neill's Va. Vetusta. Richmond, Va., Standard, II.

Bassett. Oliver's Carter Tree. Keith's Harrison Ancestry. Wm. and Mary Quar., II, V, VI, VII, XVI. Va. Hist. Mag., I, II, IV, VII. St. Peter's Par. Reg., Va. Va. Co. Records, V.

Batchelder. Middlesex Par. Reg. Va. Wm. and Mary Quar., III.

Batcheldor. Va. Co. Records, V.

Bateman. Gray's Hist. of McGavock Family, 1903.

Bates. Richmond, Va., Standard, II. Wm. and Mary Quar., VI, VIII, XI. Goodwyn's Hist. of Bruton Church, Va. White's Walker Family, 1902.

Bathurst. Richmond, Va., Standard, III. Jones' Hist. of Capt. Roger Jones of Va., 1891. Wm. and Mary Quar., II, VIII, XII. Va. Co. Records, V.

Batt or Batte. Richmond, Va., Standard, III. Slaughter's Hist. of Bristol Par., Va. Wm. and Mary Quar., I. Tyler's Cradle of the Republic. Chamberlyne's Bristol Par. Reg. Va. Co. Records, V, VI.

Battaile. Va. Hist. Mag., III, IX. Va. Co. Records, I. Wm. and Mary Quar., V.

Batten. Wm. and Mary Quar., IV.

Battle. Wheeler's History of No. Carolina.

Baugh. Va. Hist. Mag., VII. Chamberlyne's Bristol Par. Reg., 1898. Va. Co. Records, VI.

Bayard. Wm. and Mary Quar., VIII.

Baylor. Meade's Old Fam. and Churches of Va. Page Family of Va., by R. C. M. Page, 1883. Va. Hist. Mag., VI. Va. Co. Records, I. Wm. and Mary Quar., X. Stubbs' Descendants of Mordecai Cooke, 1896.

Bayly. Wm. and Mary Quar., VII.

Bayne. Va. Co. Records, VI. Wm. and Mary Quar., XIII.

Baytop. Richmond, Va., Standard, III. Va. Hist. Mag., XI. Wm. and Mary Quar., II. Descendants of Mordecai Cooke, by Stubbs.

Beach. Wm. and Mary Quar., XVIII.

Beale. Wm. and Mary Quar., I, III, XI, XIII. Va. Hist. Mag., VII. Va. Co., Records, V, VI. Warfield's Founders of Anne Arundel and Howard Cos., Md. The Brooke Fam. of Maryland, by Thos. W. Balch, 1898.

Beard. Warfield's Founders of Anne Arundel and Howard Cos., Md. Wm. and Mary Quar., XII.

Beasley. Va. Co. Records, I.

Beck. Goode's Va. Cousins. Chamberlyne's Bristol Par. Reg., 1898.

Beckwith. Slaughter's Bristol Par., Va. Va. Hist. Mag., VII. Wm. and Mary Quar., XIV. Va. Co. Records, V. VI.

Bedinger. Lee of Va., by E. J. Lee, 1895.

Bedon. Bulloch Family, by J. G. Bulloch, 1892.

Beheathland. Va. Hist. Mag., XI.

Belcher. Chamberlyne's Bristol Par. Reg. Goode's Va. Cousins.

Belfield. Richmond, Va., Standard, IV. Jones' Gen., by L. H. Jones.

Bell. Peyton's Augusta Co., Va. Richmond, Va., Standard, III. Slaughter's St. Mark's Par. Va. Co. Records, I, II, VI, VII. Goodwyn's Hist. of Bruton Church, Va. Wm. and Mary Quar., IX. The Buford Family, by M. B. Buford, 1903. Paxton's Marshall Family. Bell Family of Maryland, 1894.

Benger. Va. Hist. Mag., II. Va. Co. Records, I.

Benn. Wm. and Mary Quar., VII.

Bennett. Warfield's Founders of Anne Arundel Co., Md. Gen. of the Bennett Fam. of Md., by B. B. Browne, 1894. Neill's Va. Carolorum. Slaughter's St. Mark's Par. MSS. Pedigree at Va. Hist. Society, Richmond. Va. Hist. Mag., III, VI. Wm. and Mary Quar., III, VII, X, XIII. Middlesex Par. Reg., Va. Va. Co. Records, II, V, VI. Tyler's Cradle of the Republic.

Benthall. Va. Co. Records, VI.

Bentley. Va. Co. Records, IV, VI. Robertson's Pocahontas' Descendants.

Benton. Peyton's Hist. of Augusta Co., Va. Richmond, Va. Standard, II.

Berkeley. Oliver's Carter Pedigree. Page Family, by R. C. M. Page. Richmond, Va., Standard, I, III, IV. Wm. and Mary Quar., II, V, VI, VII. Va. Hist. Mag., XV. Middlesex Par. Reg., Va. Richmond Critic, 6th Dec., 1890.

Bernard. Richmond, Va., Standard, III. Robertson's Pocahontas' Descendants. Wm. and Mary Quar., IV, V. Va. Hist. Mag., IV, VI. Va. Hist. Collections, V. Crozier's History of the Buckner Family of Va., 1907. Va. Co. Records, IV, V, VI. White's Hist. of the Walker Fam. of Va., 1902.

Berry. Va. Co. Records, I, VI. Middlesex, Va., Par. Reg. Bowies and Their Kin, by W. W. Bowie, 1899.

Berryman. Va. Co. Records, I. IV, VI.

Bertrand. Hayden's Va. Gen. Va. Hist. Collections, V.

Best. Wm. and Mary Quar., VII.

Beverley. Oliver's Carter Fam. Tree. Neill's Va. Carolorum. Meade's Old Fam. and Churches of Va., II. Va. Hist. Mag., II, III. Wm. and Mary Quar., II, VI, XVII. Va. Co. Records, I, V, VI. Middlesex, Va., Par. Reg. Lee of Va., by E. J. Lee, 1895.

Bibb. Wood's Hist. of Albemarle, Va. Saunder's Early Settlers of Ala., 1899. Gilmer's Georgians, 1855.

Bickley. Wm. and Mary Quar., IV, V, IX, X. Va. Hist. Mag., XI. Va. Co. Records, V.

Biggs. Va. Hist. Mag., XI.

Billington. Hayden's Va. Gen.

Billups. Saunder's Early Settlers of Ala., 1899.

Binford. Wm. and Mary Quar., V.

Birchett. Chamberlyne's Bristol Par. Reg., 1898.

Birney. Green's Kentucky Families, 1889.

Bishop. Wood's History of Albemarle Co., Va. Wm. and Mary Quar., III.

Black. Slaughter's Hist. of Bristol Par., Va. Wood's Hist. of Albemarle Co., Va. Wm. and Mary Quar., VIII. Hanson's Hist. of Old Kent, Md., 1876.

Blackburn. Hayden's Va. Gen. Meade's Old Fam. and Churches, II. Paxton's Marshall Gen. Wm. and Mary Quar., IV. The Thomas Book, by L. B. Thomas, 1896. Middlesex Par. Reg., Va. Va. Co. Records, VI, VII. The Buford Family, by M. B. Buford, 1903.

Blackford. Paxton's Marshall Gen.

Blackman. Wm. and Mary Quar., VI. Chamberlyne's Bristol Par. Reg.

Blackwell. Hayden's Va. Gen. Wm. and Mary Quar., XV. Va. Co. Records, VI, VII.

Bladen. Maryland Hist. Mag., V.

Blaikley. Goodwyn's Hist. of Bruton Church, Va. Wm. and Mary Quar., II.

Blair. Page Gen., by R. C. M. Page. Richmond, Va., Standard, II. Wm. and Mary Quar., I, V, VII, VIII, XVII. Va. Hist. Mag., IV. Va. Co. Records, I, II, VI, VII. Goodwyn's Hist. of Bruton Church, Va. Horner's Hist. of the Blair Fam., 1898. Saunder's Early Settlers of Ala., 1899. Green's Kentucky Families.

Blake. Middlesex Par. Reg., Va. Va. Co. Records, VI. So. Carolina Hist. Mag., I.

Blakey. Middlesex Par. Reg., Va. Wm. and Mary Quar., IX.

Blakistone. Maryland Hist. Mag., II.

Bland. Bland Papers. Campbell's Hist. of Va. Goode's Va. Cousins. Meade's Old Fam. and Churches of Va., I. New Eng. Hist. Reg., XXXVI. Robertson's Pocahontas' Descendants. Richmond, Va., Critic, 9th July, 1888. Richmond, Va., Standard, II, III. Slaughter's Bristol Par., Va. Va. Hist. Mag., III, IV, IX, X. Middlesex Par. Reg., Va. Va. Hist. Collections, V. Goodwyn's Hist. of Bruton Church, Va. Wm. and Mary Quar., III, IV, V, VII, VIII, XVII. Chamberlyne's Bristol Par. Reg., Va. Va. Co. Records, V, VI. Lee of Va., by E. J. Lee, 1895.

Blanton. Va. Co. Records, I.

Blay. Hanson's Hist. of Old Kent, Md.

Blaydes. Va. Co. Records, I.

Bledsoe. Va. Co. Records, I, II. Hist. of Southwest Va., by L. P. Summers, 1903. Va. Hist. Mag., VI, VII. Historic Sumner County, Tenn., by Jay G. Cisco, Nashville, 1909.

Blood. Wm. and Mary Quar., VI.

Bloomfield. Va. Co. Records, VI.

Blount. Va. Hist. Mag., V.

Blow. Wm. and Mary Quar., IV.

Blunt. Va. Hist. Mag., V. Middlesex, Va., Par. Reg.

Boggs. Hayden's Va. Gen.

Bohannon. Wm. and Mary Quar., VI. Va. Co. Records, I. Middlesex Par. Reg.

Boisseau. Wm. and Mary Quar., V, IX, XIV. Chamberlayne's Bristol Par. Reg.

Boldero. Wm. and Mary Quar., IV.

Bolling. The Bolling Fam. in England and Va., by Robert Bolling, 1868. Goode's Va. Cousins. Hayden's Va. Gen. Meade's Old Fam. and Churches. New Eng. Genl. and Hist. Reg., XXVI. Richmond, Va., Standard, II, III. Robertson's Pocahontas' Descendants. Slaughter's Hist. of Bristol Par., Va. Va. Hist. Mag., VII. Goodwyn's Hist. of Bruton Church, Va. Wm. and Mary Quar., V, VIII, XVII, XVIII. Chamberlayne's Bristol Par., Va., Reg. Va. Co. Records, V, VI. Lee of Va., by E. J. Lee, 1895. MSS. Ped. of the Genealogical Assn.

Bolton. St. Peter's Par. Reg., New Kent., Va. Va. Co. Records, II.

Bond. Hayden's Va. Gen. Goodwyn's Hist. of Bruton Church, Va. Wm. and Mary Quar., VII. MSS. Ped. of the Genealogical Assn.

Bondurant. Va. Hist. Collections, V.

Bonnell. Tyler's Cradle of the Republic, 1906.

Bonner. Chamberlayne's Bristol Par. Reg., Va.

Bonney. Lower Norfolk Co., Va., Antiquary.

Booker. Wm. and Mary Quar., VII. Va. Hist. Mag., VII. Va. Co. Records, IV.

Boone. Slaughter's Hist. of St. Mark's Par., Va. Walker Fam. of Va., by Emma S. White, 1902. Woods-McAfee Memorial, by Woods and Durett, 1905.

Booth. Wm. and Mary Quar., II, III, V, VI, XI. Va. Hist. Mag., III. Goodwyn's Hist. of Bruton Church, Va. Va. Co. Records, V, VI. Descendants of Mordecai Cooke, Va., by W. C. Stubbs, 1896.

Borden. Woods-McAfee Memorial, by Woods and Durett, 1905. Wm. and Mary Quar., V.

Bordley. Hanson's Hist. of Old Kent., Md., 1876. Bordley Fam. of Maryland, by Mrs. E. B. Gibson, 1865.

Bostwick. Bostwick Fam. in America, by H. A. Bostwick, 1901.

Boswell. Wm. and Mary Quar., VIII. Va. Co. Records, I, VI. MSS. Ped. of Genealogical Assn.

Bouldin. Goode's Va. Cousins. Hayden's Va. Gen. Richmond, Va., Standard, III. Wm. and Mary Quar., V, XII.

Boush. Wm. and Mary Quar., II. Va. Co. Records, VI. Lower Norfolk Co., Va., Antiquary.

Bowcock. Wood's Hist. of Albemarle Co., Va.

Bowdoin. Meade's Old Fam. and Churches. Wm. and Mary Quar., IV.

Bowen. Va. Co. Records, II, VI. Chamberlayne's Bristol Par. Reg., Va. Green's Hist. of Culpeper Co., Va. Summer's Hist. of Washington Co., Va. Wood's Hist. of Albemarle Co., Va. Middlesex, Va., Par. Reg.

Bowie. Slaughter's Hist. of St. Mark's Par., Va. The Bowies and Their Kin, by W. W. Bowie, 1899. Va. Hist. Mag., X. Wm. and Mary Quar., X. Va. Co. Records, V. Warfield's Founders of Anne Arundel and Howard Cos., Md. MSS. Ped. of the Genealogical Assn.

Bowker. Va. Hist. Mag., XI. Va. Co. Records, I.

Bowler. Wm. and Mary Quar., VI. Va. Co. Records, VI.

Bowles. Va. Hist. Mag., XVI. Middlesex, Va., Par. Reg. St. Peter's Par. Reg., New Kent, Va. Wm. and Mary Quar., IX. Va. Co. Records, V. Hist. of the Bowles Fam., by T. M. Farquahar.

Bowman. Va. Co. Records, II. Green's Kentucky Families, 1889.

Bowne. The Thomas Fam., of Md., by L. B. Thomas.

Bowyer. Va. Co. Records, II, VI. Wm. and Mary Quar., II. Woods-McAfee Memorial, by Woods and Durett, 1905. Johnson's Memorials of Old Va. Clerks, 1888.

Box. Habersham Hist. Coll. Ga., I.

Boyd. Goode's Va. Cousins. Richmond, Va., Standard, III. Wm. and Mary Quar., VII. Va. Co. Records, II.

Boyse. Va. Hist. Mag., IV.

Bracewell. Wm. and Mary Quar., VII.

Bradburn. Va. Co. Records, I.

Bradford. Slaughter's Hist. of St. Mark's Par., Va. Va. Co. Records, VI. Anderson's Robertson Genealogy, 1900.

Bradley. Meade's Old Fam. and Churches. Va. Co. Records, I, II. Middlesex, Va., Par. Reg. St. Peter's Par. Reg., New Kent, Va.

Bradshaw. Va. Hist. Mag., V.

Bragdon. Eminent North Carolinians, by J. W. Wheeler, 1884.

Branch. Goode's Va. Cousins. Meade's Old Fam. and Churches. Robertson's Pocahontas' Descendants. Middlesex, Va., Par. Reg. Wm. and Mary Quar., VII, IX. Hist. of the Branch Fam., by Jas. B. Cabell, 1907. Richmond, Va., Critic, 2d Nov., 1899. Va. Co. Records, V, VI.

Brand. Wood's Hist. of Albemarle, Va. Va. Co. Records, IV.

Branham. Va. Co. Records, I, II. Va. Hist. Collections, V.

Branner. Branner Fam. of Va., by J. C. Branner, 1904.

Brannin. Va. Hist. Mag., V.

Brantley. Wm. and Mary Quar., VII.

Braxton. Hist. of the Spotswood Fam. of Va., by Charles Campbell, 1868. Oliver's Carter Pedigree. Meade's Old Fam. and Churches. Richmond, Va., Standard, III. Va. Hist. Mag., VI. Wm. and Mary Quar., IV. History of the Blair, Banister and Braxton Families, by F. Horner, 1898.

Bray. Va. Hist. Mag., XI. Wm. and Mary Quar., V, VI, VII, XIII, XIV. Middlesex, Va., Par. Reg. Va. Hist. Collections, V. Goodwyn's Hist. of Bruton Church, Va. Va. Co. Records, I, V.

Brayne. Wm. and Mary Quar., X.

Brecht. Habersham Hist. Collections Ga., I.

Breckenridge. Meade's Old Fam. and Churches. Paxton's Marshall Gen. Peyton's Hist. of Augusta Co., Va. The Preston Family, by W. B. Preston, 1900. Richmond, Va., Standard, II. Va. Hist. Mag., X. Green's Kentucky Families. Hist. of Kentucky, by Lewis Collins, 1847. Va. Co. Records, II.

Brent. Goode's Va. Cousins. Meade's Old Fam. and Churches. Paxton's Marshall Gen. Richmond, Va., Critic, 17th Mar., 1899. Richmond, Va., Standard, II. Va. Hist. Mag., I, II, VIII, XI, XII, XIII, XIV, XV, XVI, XVII, XVIII. Wm. and Mary Quar., I, IV. Va. Co. Records, V, VI, VII. Hanson's Hist. of Old Kent, Md.

Brereton. Wm. and Mary Quar., IV, IX.

Bressie. Wm. and Mary Quar., VII.

Brett. Richmond, Va., Standard, III. Wm. and Mary Quar., I.

Brewer. Va. Hist. Mag., III. Va. Co. Records, VI.

Brewster. Wm. and Mary Quar., IV. Va. Co. Records, VI. Some Notable Families of America, by Annah R. Watson, 1898.

ewton. So. Car. Genl. and Hist. Mag., II.

Brice. Va. Hist. Mag., V. Hanson's Hist. of Old Kent, Md. Warfield's Hist. of Anne Arundel and Howard Cos., Md.

Bridge. Wm. and Mary Quar., XV.

Bridger. Meade's Old Fam. and Churches. Richmond, Va., Standard,
II, III. Va. Hist. Mag., II. Wm. and Mary Quar., VII. Va. Co.
Records, II, VI.

Bridges. Va. Hist. Collections, V.

Briggs. Va. Co. Records, II. St. Peter's Par. Reg., New Kent Co., Va.

Bright. Richmond, Va., Standard, III. Wm. and Mary Quar., XII.
Habersham Hist. Coll. Ga., I. Va. Co. Records, II.

Briscoe. Hayden's Va. Gen. Hanson's Hist. of Old Kent, Md.

Bristow. Va. Hist. Mag., XIII. Middlesex, Va., Par. Reg. Wm.
and Mary Quar., II. Va. Co. Records, II, V.

Broadhead. Va. Hist. Mag., III.

Broadhurst. Wm. and Mary Quar., I, IV.

Broadnax. Meade's Old Fam. and Churches. Slaughter's Hist. of
Bristol Par., Va. Wm. and Mary Quar., XIV.

Broadus. Slaughter's Hist. of St. Mark's Par., Va. Green's Hist. of
Culpeper Co., Va.

Brock. Munsell's American Ancestry, VII. Va. Co. Records, I, II.
Lower Norfolk Co., Va., Antiquary.

Brockenbrough. Goode's Va. Cousins. Hayden's Va. Gen. Meade's
Old Fam. and Churches. Paxton's Marshall Gen. Richmond, Va.,
Standard, II, III. Wm. and Mary Quar., XI. Va. Hist. Mag.,
V, VI.

Brockman. Wood's Hist. of Albemarle Co., Va.

Brodhurst. Wm. and Mary Quar., XVII. Va. Hist. Mag., XVII.

Brodnax. Wm. and Mary Quar., VI, XIV. Va. Co. Records, V.

Brogden. Hanson's Hist. of Old Kent, Md. Eminent North Carolinians, by J. H. Wheeler, 1884.

Bronaugh. Hayden's Va. Gen. Wm. and Mary Quar., XVII. Va.
Co. Records, I, II, IV.

Brooke. Goode's Va. Cousins. Meade's Old Fam. and Churches. Page
Gen., by R. C. M. Page, 1883. Paxton's Marshall Gen. Thomas
Family of Md., by L. B. Thomas. Wm. and Mary Quar., IV, VI,
IX, XI. MSS. Coll. of Va. Hist. Society, File A. Va. Hist. Mag.,
I, II, IX, X, XI, XII, XIII, XV, XVI, XVII, XVIII. Va. Co.
Records, I, II. The Bowies and Their Kin, by W. W. Bowie, 1899.
Warfield's Hist. of Anne Arundel and Howard Cos., Md. The
Thomas Book, by I. B. Thomas, 1896. The Brooke Fam. of Md.
(Chart), by B. B. Browne, 1894. The Brooke Fam. of Md., by
Thos. W. Balch, 1898.

Brookes. Wm. and Mary Quar., VII. Va. Co. Records, VI. Wood's
Hist. of Albemarle Co., Va. Chamberlayne's Bristol Par. Reg., Va.

Broughton. Wm. and Mary Quar., XV. Va. Co. Records, II.

Broun. Va. Hist. Mag., XVII. Wm. and Mary Quar., IX, XIII.
Walker Fam. of Va., by Emma S. White, 1902.

Brown. Oliver's Carter Fam. of Va. Foote's Sketches of Va., 2d Series. Hayden's Va. Gen. Peyton's Hist. of Augusta Co., Va. Richmond, Va., Standard, II, III. Green's Hist. of Culpeper Co., Va. Wood's Hist. of Albemarle Co., Va. Wm. and Mary Quar., IV, IX, XII, XIII. Va. Co. Records, I, II, VI. The Lower Norfolk Co., Va., Antiquary. Chamberlayne's Bristol Par. Reg., Va. Brown Fam. of Prince William Co., Va., by Jas. E. Brown, 1898.

Browne. Meade's Old Fam. and Churches. Richmond, Va., Standard, II, III. Slaughter's Hist. of Bristol Par., Va. MSS. Ped. of Va. Hist. Society, File A. Wm. and Mary Quar., IV, V, VI, VII, VIII, XVI. Va. Hist. Mag., III, V. Va. Co. Records, III, V, VI. Browne Fam. of Maryland, by B. B. Browne (sheet), 1894. Warfield's Hist. of Anne Arundel and Howard Cos., Md. Munsell's American Ancestry, VII.

Browning. Green's Hist. of Culpeper Co., Va. Jones Fam. of Va., by Lewis H. Jones, 1891. Crozier's Hist. of the Buckners of Va. McAllister and Tandy's Hist. of the Lewis Fam., 1906. The Browning Fam. in America, by E. F. Browning, 1908.

Bruce. Richmond, Va., Standard, II. Va. Hist. Mag., XI, XII. Wm. and Mary Quar., VI. Woods-McAfee Memorial, by Woods and Durett, 1905.

Bryan. Hayden's Va. Gen. Slaughter's Hist. of Bristol Par., Va. Green's Hist. of Culpeper Co., Va. Goodwyn's Hist. of Bruton Church, Va. Wm. and Mary Quar., V. Habersham Hist. Coll. Ga., I, II. Va. Co. Records, II.

Buchanan. Va. Co. Records, II.

Buck. Middlesex Par. Reg., Va. Wm. and Mary Quar., VII.

Buckingham. Wm. and Mary Quar., I.

Buckley. The Thomas Family of Md., by L. B. Thomas.

Buckner. Goode's Va. Cousins. Meade's Old Fam. and Churches. Va. Hist. Mag., IV, V, VI, XI. Wm. and Mary Quar., V, VI, VII, XIV. Richmond, Va., Critic, 1890. Va. Co. Records, I, II, V, VI. Crozier's Hist. of the Buckner Fam. of Va., 1907. The Descendants of Mordecai Cooke of Va., by W. C. Stubbs, 1896. Gibbons-Butcher Genealogy, by A. F. Gibbons, 1894. The Reminiscences of the Buckner Family, by Katherine E. Tuley, 1901.

Buford. Paxton's Marshall Gen. The Buford Fam., by M. B. Buford, 1903. The McGavock Fam., by Rev. Robert Gray, 1903. Green's Kentucky Families. Va. Co. Records, II.

Bugg. Wm. and Mary Quar., X, XI.

Bull. Hayden's Va. Gen. So. Car. Hist. Mag., I.

Bullard. Va. Co. Records, I, II.

Bullington. Neill's Va. Carolorum. Va. Co. Records, VI.

Bullitt. Hayden's Va. Gen. Richmond, Va., Standard, III. Slaughter's Fry Gen. Green's Kentucky Families. Va. Co. Records, II.

Bulloch. Habersham Hist. Coll. of Ga., I. Munsell's American Ancestry, VII. History of the Bulloch Fam., by J. G. Bulloch.

Bullock. Va. Hist. Mag., II. Va. Co. Records, I, VI.

Burbage. Va. Hist. Mag., V.

Burbank. Slaughter's Hist. of St. Mark's Par., Va.

Burbridge. Va. Co. Records, I.

Burch. Wood's Hist. of Albemarle Co., Va.

Burden. Green's Kentucky Families.

Burdett. Va. Hist. Mag., II. Wm. and Mary Quar., I, VII.

Burgess. Warfield's Founders of Anne Arundel and Howard Cos., Md. Wm. and Mary Quar., VI.

Burgwin. Munsell's American Ancestry, VII.

Burke. Wm. and Mary Quar., XI. Va. Co. Records, II.

Burnell. Wm. and Mary Quar., VII.

Burnett. Wm. and Mary Quar., V, VI, VII.

Burnham. Va. Hist. Mag., I. Wm. and Mary Quar., II.

Burnely. Wood's Hist. of Albemarle Co., Va.

Burroughs. Va. Hist. Mag., V.

Burton. Wm. and Mary Quar., V, XI. Chamberlayne's Bristol Par. Reg. Va. Co. Records, II, VI. Wheeler's Hist. of No. Carolina, 1851.

Burwell. Campbell's Hist. of Va. Oliver's Carter Pedigree. Goode's Va. Cousins. Meade's Old Fam. and Churches. Page Gen., by R. C. M. Page, 1883. Paxton's Marshall Gen. Richmond, Va., Standard, I, II, III, IV. Wm. and Mary Quar., I, II, III, IV, V, VI, VII, XIV, XV. Va. Hist. Mag., II, V. Keith's Harrison Ancestry, 1893. Middlesex Par. Reg., Va. Hist. of Bruton Church, Va. Tyler's Cradle of the Republic, 1906. Va. Co. Records, V.

Bush. Paxton's Marshall Gen. The Gentry Fam. in America, by R. Gentry, 1909. The Quisenberry Fam., by A. C. Quisenberry, 1900.

Bushrod. Hayden's Va. Gen. Wm. and Mary Quar., I, VII, XIV, XVII.

Butcher. Gibbons-Butcher Genealogy, by A. F. Gibbens, 1894.

Butler. Meade's Old Fam. and Churches. Paxton's Marshall Gen. Va. Hist. Mag., XI. Va. Co. Records, I, V, VI, VII. Wm. and Mary Quar., VIII. Chamberlayne's Bristol Par. Reg. The Woods-McAfee Memorial, by Woods and Durett, 1905. Green's Kentucky Families. So. Carolina Hist. Mag., IV.

Butt. Va. Co. Records, VI. Lower Norfolk Co., Va., Antiquary.

Butters. The Butters Family in the U. S., with the Va. Branch, by Geo. Butters, 1896.

Byrd. Campbell's Hist. of Va. Meade's Old Fam. and Churches. Balch's Provincial Papers. New Eng. Hist. and Genl. Register, XXXIV, XXXVIII. Paxton's Marshall Gen. Page Genealogy, by R. C. M. Page. Richmond, Va., Critic, 16th Dec., 1888. Sketches and Recollections of Lynchburg, by Mrs. Julia M. Cabell, 1858. Slaughter's Hist. of Bristol Parish, Va. Va. Hist. Mag., VI, IX. Va. Hist. Collections, V. Wm. and Mary Quar., III, IV, VIII, IX, XIII. Habersham Hist. Collections Ga., I. Va. Co. Records, II, V. The Westover Estate, Harper's Mag., Vol. 42.

Cabell. Meade's Old Fam. and Churches. Campbell's Hist. of Va. Sketches and Recollections of Lynchburg, by Mrs. Julia M. Cabell, 1858. Robertson's Pocahontas' Descendants. Slaughter's Fry Genealogy. The Cabells and Their Kin, by Alex. Brown, 1895. Wm. and Mary Quar., IV. Va. Co. Records, V.

Caldwell. Richmond, Va., Standard II. Habersham Hist. Coll. of Ga., I. Va. Co. Records, II.

Calhoun. So. Carolina Hist. Mag., VII. Calhoun Fam. of So. Car., by A. S. Salley, Jr., 1906.

Callaway. Meade's Old Fam. and Churches. Richmond, Va., Standard, I. Habersham Hist. Coll. of Ga., I. Wm. and Mary Quar., III, XIII.

Calmes. Habersham Hist. Coll. of Ga., I.

Calthorpe. Wm. and Mary Quar., II, XIV. Va. Co. Records, V.

Calvert. Neill's Terra Mariae. Richmond, Va., Standard, III. Va. Hist. Mag., V, VI. Va. Co. Records, III, V, VI. Wm. and Mary Quar., IV. Lower Norfolk Co., Va., Antiquary. Maryland Hist. Mag., II.

Cameron. Johnston's Memorials of Old Va. Clerks, 1888.

Camm. Wm. and Mary Quar., III, IV, VIII, XIV. Va. Co. Records, V.

Cammack. Va. Co. Records, I.

Camp. Va. Hist. Mag., IX.

Campbell. Foote's Sketches of Va., 2d Series. Hayden's Va. Gen. Meade's Old Fam. and Churches. Peyton's Hist. of Augusta Co., Va. Richmond, Va., Standard, I, II, III, IV. Slaughter's Hist. of St. Mark's Par. Va. Hist. Mag., VI, VII. Va. Co. Records, I, II, III, VI, VII. Wm. and Mary Quar., VII. Hist. of So. West Va., by L. P. Summers, 1903. Paxton's Marshall Family.

Candler. Munsell's American Ancestry, VII. Col. William Candler of Georgia, and His Ancestry, by Allen D. Candler, 1902.

Cannon. Lower Norfolk Co. Antiquary.

Cant. Va. Hist. Mag., III.

Capehart. Eminent North Carolinians, by John H. Wheeler, 1884.

Capers. Habersham Hist. Coll. of Ga., I. So. Carolina Hist. Mag., II.

Capps. Wm. and Mary Quar., VI. Lower Norfolk Co., Va., Anti quary.

Carey. The Thomas Book, by L. B. Thomas, 1896.

Carle. Hanson's Hist. of Old Kent, Md.

Carlin. Goode's Va. Cousins.

Carlisle. Wm. and Mary Quar., XVIII. Va. Co. Records, II.

Carpenter. Va. County Records, I, II, VI, VII.

Carr. Meade's Old Fam. and Churches. Richmond, Va., Standard, III. Va. Hist. Mag., II, III, V. Wm. and Mary Quar., VIII. Wood's Hist. of Albemarle, Va. Va. Co. Records, I, II. The Carr Family, by Edwin L. Carr, 1894.

Carrington. Campbell's Hist. of Va. Foote's Sketches of Va., 2d Series. Goode's Va. Cousins. Meade's Old Fam. and Churches. Paxton's Marshall Gen. Richmond, Va., Standard, I, II, III. Slaughter's Hist. of St. Mark's Par., Va. Johnston's Old Va. Clerks. Wm. and Mary Quar., I. Va. Co. Records, V, VI. Green's Kentucky Families. The Cabells and Their Kin, by Alex Brown, 1895.

Carroll. Lee of Va., by E. J. Lee, 1895. Warfield's Founders of Anne Arundel and Howard Cos., Md. The Thomas Book, by L. B. Thomas. Hanson's Hist. of Old Kent, Md. Va. Co, Records, II.

Carson. Green's Kentucky Families. Eminent North Carolinians, by J. H. Wheeler, 1884.

Carter. Wm. and Mary Quar., I, III, V, VI, VIII, IX, X, XIII, XVII, XVIII, XIX. Va. Hist. Mag., II, IV, V, VI. Green's Hist. of Culpeper Co., Va. Jones Gen., by Lewis H. Jones, 1891. Wood's Hist. of Albemarle, Va. Va. Co, Records, I, II, V. Middlesex, Va., Par. Reg. St. Peter's, New Kent, Va., Par. Reg. Keith's Harrison Ancestry. Lee of Va., by E. J. Lee. Campbell's Spotswood Papers. Campbell's Hist. of Va. Carter Fam. Tree, by M. E. Oliver, 1897. Hayden's Va. Gen. Meade's Old Fam. and Churches. Richmond, Va., Critic, June-July, 1888. Richmond, Va., Standard, II, III, IV. Slaughter's Hist. of St. Mark's Par., Va. Some Colonial Mansions, I, by T. A. Glenn, 1898. Giles Carter of Va., by General W. G. H. Carter, 1909.

Carthrae. Green's Kentucky Families.

Caruthers. Richmond, Va., Standard, III. Green's Kentucky Families. Paxton's Marshall Gen.

Carver. Wm. and Mary Quar,, III.

Cary. Goode's Va. Cousins. Keith's Harrison Ancestry. Meade's Old Fam. and Churches. Richmond, Va., Critic, 26th April, 1890. Richmond, Va., Standard, II, III. Robertson's Pocahontas Descendants, Southern Bivouac, May, 1886. Va. Hist. Mag., V, VIII, IX, X. Wm. and Mary Quar., III, V, VI, IX, XV. Va. Co. Records, III, IV, V, VI. Hist. of Bruton Church, Va.

Cason. Va. Co, Records, I. The Lower Norfolk Co., Va., Antiquary. Eminent North Carolinians, by J. H. Wheeler, 1884.

Catesby. Richmond, Va., Standard, II. Jones Fam., by L. H. Jones, 1891.

Catlett. Oliver's Carter Fam. Hayden's Va. Gen. Meade's Old Fam. and Churches. Slaughter's Hist. of St. Mark's Par., Va. Habersham Hist, Coll. of Ga., I. Va. Hist. Mag., III, V. Va. Co. Records, I, VI.

Catlin. Warfield's Hist. of Anne Arundel and Howard Cos., Md., 1905.

Caufield. Wm. and Mary Quar., VII.

Cave. Hayden's Va. Gen. Slaughter's Hist. of St. Mark's Par. Green's Hist, of Culpeper Co., Va. Va. Co. Records, I, II.

Cay. Va. Co. Records, V.

Cazenove. Va. Hist, Coll. V.

Chamberlain. Meade's Old Fam. and Churches. Va. Hist. Mag., VI. St. Peter's Par. Reg., New Kent Co., Va. Wm. and Mary Quar., I, V. Va. Co. Records, VI, VII. Hanson's Hist. of Old Kent, Md. Chamberlain Family of Md., by J. B. Piet, 1880.

Chambers. Va. Co. Records, VI, VII. Lee of Va., by E. J. Lee, 1895.

Champe. Richmond, Va., Standard, III. Va. Co. Records, I. The Willis Fam. of Va., by B. C. and H. Willis.

Champion. Wm. and Mary Quar., VII.

VIRGINIA COUNTY RECORDS. 17

Chandler. Va. Hist. Mag., III. Va. Co. Records, I, VI. St. Peter's Par. Reg., New Kent, Va. Chamberlayne's Bristol Par. Reg., Va.

Chapline. Chaplines from Maryland and Va., by Maria J. L. Dare, 1902.

Chapman. Goode's Va. Cousins. Richmond, Va., Standard, II, III. Wm. and Mary Quar., IV, V, VI, VII, X, XIX. Va. Hist. Mag., IX. Va. Co. Records, I, II, V, VI, VII.

Chappell. Chappell, Dickie and Other Families of Va., by Philip E. Chappell, 1900. Va. Hist. Mag., III. Chamberlayne's Bristol Par. Va., Reg. St. Peter's Par. Reg., New Kent Co., Va.

Charlton. Va. Co. Records, II, VI.

Chase. Warfield's Hist. of Anne Arundel and Howard Cos., Md.

Chastain. Va. Hist. Collections, V.

Chenault. Habersham Hist. Coll. of Ga., I.

Chenoweth. The Chenoweth and Cromwell Families of Md. and Va., by A. C. Chenoweth, 1894.

Cheesman. Va. Hist. Mag., I.

Chesley. Va. Hist. Mag., XIII. Paxton's Marshall Family.

Chew. Richmond, Va., Critic, 1888. The Thomas Book, by L. B. Thomas, 1896. Va. Hist. Mag., I, II, III, V, VI. Va. Co. Records, I, II, V. Warfield's Hist. of Anne Arundel and Howard Cos., Md. The Bowies and Their Kin, by W. W. Bowie, 1899.

Chicheley. Va. Hist. Mag., III, XVII. Wm. and Mary Quar., II. Va. Co. Records, V.

Chichester. Hayden's Va. Gen. Wm. and Mary Quar., XVII. Va. Co. Records, V.

Childers. Va. Co. Records, VI, VII.

Childress. Chamberlayne's Bristol Par. Reg., Va.

Chiles. Wm. and Mary Quar., I, VI, VIII, XVI, XVII, XVIII. Va. Co. Records, I, VI.

Chilton. Wm. and Mary Quar., X, XV. Va. Co. Records, VI.

Chinn. Hayden's Va. Gen.

Chisman. Wm. and Mary Quar., I, II, XIII, XIV. Va. Hist. Mag., XIV.

Chiswell. Wm. and Mary Quar., I, IX.

Chowning. Middlesex, Va., Par. Reg.

Chrisman. Green's Kentucky Families.

Christian. Meade's Old Fam. and Churches. Peyton's Hist. of Augusta Co., Va. Slaughter's Hist. of St. Mark's Par., Va. Johnson's Old Va. Clerks. Wm. and Mary Quar., V, VII, VIII, IX, X, XV, XVIII. Va. Hist. Mag., II, VIII. Va. Co. Records, II, III. St. Peter's Par. Reg., New Kent Co., Va. Letters and Times of the Tylers, by Lyon G. Tyler, 1897. Green's Kentucky Families.

Churchill. Hayden's Va. Gen. Wm. and Mary Quar., VII, VIII, IX, X. Va. Hist. Mag., VIII, XVI. Middlesex, Va., Par. Reg. Va. Co., Records, V. Keith's Harrison Ancestry.

Cissel. Warfield's Hist. of Anne Arundel and Howard Cos., Md.

Clack. Va. Hist. Mag., VIII. Wm. and Mary Quar., IV, VII, VIII, XI, XIV, XIX.

Claflin. Hayden's Va. Gen.

Clagett. The Bowies and Their Kin, by W. W. Bowie, 1899.

Claiborne. Oliver's Carter Family Tree. Goode's Va. Cousins. Meade's Old Fam. and Churches. Neill's Va. Carolorum. Richmond, Va., Standard, II, III, IV. Slaughter's Hist. of Bristol Par., Va. Habersham Hist. Coll. of Ga., I. Claiborne Pedigree, by G. M. Claiborne, 1900. Va. Hist. Mag., I, II, V. Crozier's History of the Buckner Fam. of Va., 1907. Wm. and Mary Quar., III, V, VIII, IX. Va. Co. Records, V, VI.

Clapham. Va. Hist. Mag., XII. Va. Co. Records, VI.

Clark. Richmond, Va., Standard, III. Slaughter's Hist. of St. Mark's Par., Va., Va. Hist. Mag., III, IX. Wood's Hist. of Albemarle, Va. Va. Co. Records, I, II, VI. Wm. and Mary Quar., I, VII. Woods-McAfee Memorial, by Woods and Durett, 1905. Eminent North Carolinians, by J. H. Wheeler, 1884. The Anderson, Clark, Marshall and McArthur Families, by General T. McA. Anderson. Habersham Hist. Coll. of Ga., II.

Clarke. Goode's Va. Cousins. Meade's Old Fam. and Churches. Richmond, Va., Standard, II. Va. Co. Records, I, II, VI. St. Peter's Par. Reg., New Kent Co., Va. Va. Hist. Mag., VI. Chamberlayne's Bristol Par. Reg., Va. Green's Kentucky Families.

Clarkson. Wood's Hist. of Albemarle, Va. St. Peter's Par. Reg., New Kent Co., Va. Paxton's Marshall Family.

Clay. Va. Hist. Mag., VII. Middlesex, Va., Par. Reg. Wm. and Mary Quar., VII. Va. Co. Records, VI. Saunder Early Settlers of Alabama, 1899. Anderson's Robertson and Rogers' Gen., 1900. Green's Kentucky Families. The Descendants of Joseph Clay of Savannah, Ga., by Montgomery Cumming, 1897. The Clay Family, by Mrs. Mary R. Clay, Louisville, 1899.

Clayton. Slaughter's Hist. of St. Mark's Par., Va. Va. Hist. Mag., I, IV. Green's Hist. of Culpeper Co., Va. Va. Co. Records, I, V. Wm. and Mary Quar., II, III, IV, X, XVI. The Rootes Fam. of Va., by W. C. Torrence, 1906. Habersham Hist. Coll. of Ga., II. The Clayton Family, by H. F. Hepburn.

Cleeman. Richmond, Va., Standard, II.

Clements. Va. Co. Records, II, IV. Va. Hist. Mag., II. Chamberlayne's Bristol Par. Reg., Va.

Clendenin. Va. Co. Records, II. Clendenin Fam. by Capt. J. V. Meigs, in West Va. Hist. Mag. for July, 1904.

Clifton. Wm. and Mary Quar., VII. Va. Co. Records, II.

Clopton. Wm. and Mary Quar., V, X, XI, XVII, XVIII. St. Peter's Par. Reg., New Kent Co., Va. Va. Co. Records V.

Cleveland. The Register of Descendants of Moses Cleveland of Mass., with a Sketch of the Clevelands of Va., and the Carolinas, by J. B. Cleveland, 1881.

Coalter. Slaughter's Hist. of Bristol Par., Va.

Cobb. Richmond, Va., Standard, II. Va. Co. Records, III. Wm. and Mary Quar., VI, VII. Rootes Fam. of Va., by W. C. Torrence, 1906.

Cobbs. Slaughter's Hist. of Bristol Par., Va. The Lewis Fam. of Va., by J. M. McAllister, 1906. Va. Hist., Mag., VI.

Cochran. Peyton's Hist. of Augusta Co., Va. MSS. Coll. of Va. Hist. Society, File A. Wood's Hist. of Albemarle Co., Va. Cochran Family of Maryland, by B. B. Browne, 1894. Paxton's Marshall Family.

Cocke. Richmond, Va., Standard, II, III. Slaughter's Hist. of Bristol Par., Va. Va. Hist. Coll., V. Va. Hist. Mag., III, IV, V, X, XI. Jones Gen. of Va., by L. H. Jones, 1891. Wood's Hist. of Albemarle Co., Va. Wm. and Mary Quar., I, III, IV, VI, VIII, IX, X, XVI. Middlesex Par. Reg., Va. Va. Co. Records, II, III, V. Hanson's Hist. of Old Kent, Md. Summer's Hist. of So. West Va., 1903.

Cockerill. Wm. and Mary Quar., III.

Cockersham. Wm. and Mary Quar., VIII.

Cockrell. Richmond, Va., Standard, IV. Cockrill Gen. in Am. Hist. Mag., III, Nashville, 1898.

Codrington. Richmond, Va., Standard, II.

Coghill. The Family of Coghill, by Jas. H. Coghill, 1879.

Coke. Wm. and Mary Quar., IV, VII, XVIII. Va. Co. Records, V.

Colclough. Va. Co. Records, VI. Wm. and Mary Quar., XVII.

Colcock. Hist. of Hay Fam. of So. Carolina, by C. Colcock, 1908. So. Carolina Hist. Mag., III.

Cole. Richmond, Va., Standard, II. Va. Hist. Mag., II, IX. Wm. and Mary Quar., I, II, V, X. Wood's Hist. of Albemarle, Va. Va. Co. Records, V, VI. Middlesex, Va., Par. Reg. St. Peter's, New Kent, Va., Par. Reg. Warfield's Hist. of Anne Arundel and Howard Cos., Md.

Codd. Va. Hist. Mag. X. Notes on the Codd Fam. in MSS. Coll. at the Va. Hist. Society. Va. Co. Records, V.

Coleman. Robertson's Pocahontas' Descendants. Meade's Old Fam. and Churches. Slaughter's Bristol Par., Va. Slaughter's St. Mark's Par., Va. Green's Hist. of Culpeper Co., Va. Va. Hist. Mag., V. Goodwyn's Hist. of Bruton Church, Va. Chamberlayne's Bristol Par. Reg., Va. Early Settlers of Alabama, by J. E. Saunders, 1899. Paxton's Marshall Fam. Va. Co. Records, I, II, VI.

Coles. Meade's Old Fam. and Churches. Richmond, Va., Standard, III. Slaughter's St. Mark's Par., Va. Va. Hist. Mag., VII, XV. Wood's Hist. of Albemarle Co., Va. Wm. and Mary Quar., IV, VIII. Hist. of Henrico Par., Va., Ed. by J. S. Moore, 1904.

Colleton. So. Carolina Hist. Mag., I.

Collier. Va. Co. Records, II, VI. Wm. and Mary Quar., III, VIII, IX.

Collins. Va. Co. Records, I, II, VI.

Colquhoun. Richmond, Va., Standard, II.

Colson. Va. Co. Records, I.

Colston. Wm. and Mary Quar., III, IV. Va. Co. Records, V. Paxton's Marshall Fam. Hanson's Hist. of Old Kent, Md. Richmond, Va., Critic, 12th Nov., 1888.

Colt. Wm. and Mary Quar., V.

Colville. Wm. and Mary Quar., VI, IX.

Comegys. Hanson's Hist. of Old Kent, Md.

Conner. Va. Co. Records, VI. Hanson's Hist. of Old Kent, Md. Wheeler's Hist. of No. Carolina, 1851.

Contesse. Richmond, Va., Standard, I.

Conway. Oliver's Carter Fam. Hayden's Va. Fam. Meade's Old Fam. and Churches. Slaughter's Hist. of St. Mark's Par., Va. Green's Hist. of Culpeper Co., Va. Wm. and Mary Quar., X, XII. Va. Hist. Mag., V. Va. Co. Records, II, V, VI. Conway Fam. of Va. (Ped. Sheet), by Thos. L. Broun, 1906. Conway Fam. of Va., Richmond Times-Dispatch, Jan. 10 and 17, 1904.

Cook. Va. Co. Records, I, II, III, V, VI. Chamberlayne's Hist. of Bristol Par. Middlesex Par. Reg., Va. Descendants of Mordecai Cooke, Gloucester Co., Va., by W. C. Stubbs. St. Peter's Par. Reg., New Kent, Va. Slaughter's Hist. of St. Mark's Par., Va. Wm. and Mary Quar., II, III, V, XI. Hanson's Hist. of Old Kent, Md.

Cooper. Goode's Va. Cousins. Richmond, Va., Standard, III. Va. Hist. Mag., VI, IX. Va. Co. Records, II, VI. Lower Norfolk Co., Va., Antiquary. Middlesex, Va., Par Reg.

Copeland. Wm. and Mary Quar., VII.

Copland. Wm. and Mary Quar., XIV, XV.

Coppedge. Wm. and Mary Quar., XI.

Corbin. Oliver's Carter Fam. Tree. Meade's Old Fam. and Churches. Richmond, Va., Standard, III. Wm. and Mary Quar., III, XIV. Middlesex, Va., Par. Reg. Va. Hist. Mag., XVII. Lee of Va., by E. J. Lee, 1895. Va. Co. Records, I, V, VI. Richmond, Va., Critic, 19th Nov., 1888.

Cordell. Hayden's Va. Gen. Richmond, Va., Standard, III.

Cordery. Wm. and Mary Quar., III.

Corker. Wm. and Mary Quar., VII.

Cornick. Lower Norfolk Co., Va., Antiquary.

Corprew. Wm. and Mary Quar., II.

Cotton. Va. Hist. Mag., X. Wm. and Mary Quar., V.

Couch. Richmond, Va., Standard, I.

Coulter. Va. Hist. Mag., VI.

Councill. Wm. and Mary Quar., VII

Courtenay. Richmond, Va., Standard, III. Wm. and Mary Quar., VII

Cowies. The Va. Cowles Family, Ped. Chart, Compiled by Eugene Cowles. Wm. and Mary Quar., III, X, XVI.

Cowman. The Thomas Book, by L. B. Thomas, 1896.

Cowper. Va. Hist. Mag., VI.

Cox. Va. Hist. Mag., X. St. Peter's Par. Reg., New Kent, Va. Va. Co. Records, II, VI. Chamberlayne's Bristol Par. Reg.

Craddock. Va. Co. Records, VI.

Craig. Gleanings of Va. History, by W. F. Boogher, 1903. Va. Co. Records, I, II. Wm. and Mary Quar., X.

Craik. Slaughter's Fry Gen., 1880. Hayden's Va. Gen. Va. Co. Records, II.

Cralle. Hayden's Va. Gen.

Crane. Goode's Va. Cousins. Va. Co. Records, I.

Craven. Wood's Hist. of Albemarle Co., Va.

Crawford. Crawford of Va., by R. L. Crawford, 1883. Meade's Old Fam. and Churches. Peyton's Hist. of Augusta Co., Va. Va. Co. Records, I, V, VI. Richmond, Va., Standard, II, III. Woods-McAfee Memorial, by Woods and Durett, 1905.

Crawley. Wm. and Mary Quar., VIII.

Crenshaw. Goode's Va. Cousins. Richmond, Va., Standard, II, III.

Creyke. Va. Co. Records, V.

Crittenden. Richmond, Va., Standard, II. Middlesex, Va., Par. Reg. St. Peter's Par. Reg., New Kent, Va. Green's Kentucky Fam.

Crocker. Wm. and Mary Quar., VII.

Crockett. Peyton's Hist. of Augusta Co., Va. Va. Co. Records, II. The McGavock Family, by Rev. Robert Gray, 1903.

Cromwell. Gen. of the Chenoweth and Cromwell Families of Md. and Va., by A. C. Chenoweth, 1894.

Cropper. Johnston's Old Va. Clerks.

Croshaw. Wm. and Mary Quar., I, II, VIII. Va. Co. Records, VI.

Crouch. Richmond, Va. Standard IV.

Crowell. Wheeler's Hist. of N. Carolina. Eminent N. Carolinians, by J. H. Wheeler, 1884.

Crump. Va. Co. Records, III, VI. St. Peter's Par. Reg. New Kent, Va. Va. Hist. Mag., IV.

Crutcher. Va. Co. Records, I.

Crutchfield. Va. Co. Records, I. Middlesex, Va., Par. Reg.

Cullen. Richmond, Va., Standard, IV.

Culpeper. Va. Hist. Mag., XIV.

Cummings. Richmond, Va., Standard, III. Middlesex, Va., Par. Reg.

Cunningham. Va. Co. Records, I, II.

Cuppage. Wm. and Mary Quar., XI.

Curle. Wm. and Mary Quar., IX. Va. Co. Records, V.

Currie. Hayden's Va. Gen. Richmond, Va., Standard, V. Wm. and Mary Quar., XII. Paxton's Marshall Fam. Chamberlayne's Bristol Par. Reg.

Curtis. Meade's Old Fam. and Churches, I. Va. Hist. Mag., V. Va. Co. Records, I, II, VI. Middlesex, Va., Par. Reg. Wm. and Mary Quar., IX.

Custis. Meade's Old Fam. and Churches, I. Neill's Va. Carolorum. Richmond, Va., Standard, III. Wm. and Mary Quar., III, V. Va. Co. Records, II, V. Goodwyn's Hist. of Bruton Church, Va. St. Peter's Par. Reg., New Kent, Va. Lee of Va., by E. J. Lee. Paxton's Marshall Fam.

Cuthbert. The Cuthberts of So. Carolina and Ga., by J. G. B. Bulloch, 1908.

Cutts. Richmond, Va., Standard, III. Slaughter's Hist. of St. Mark's Par., Va.

Dabney. The Dabneys of Va., by Wm. H. Dabney, 1888. Sketches of the First Families of Upper Georgia, by G. R. Gilmer, 1855. Meade's Old Fam. and Churches. The Page Family, by R. C. M. Page, 1883. Richmond, Va., Standard, II, III. Sketches of Lynchburg, by Mrs. J. M. Cabell. Slaughter's Hist. of St. Mark's Par. Wood's Hist. of Albemarle Co., Va. Wm. and Mary Quar., IV. Va. Co. Records, VI.

Dade. Hayden's Va. Gen. Slaughter's Hist. of St. Mark's Par., Va. Wm. and Mary Quar., XII, XIII.

Daingerfield. Meade's Old Fam. and Churches, I. Richmond, Va., Standard, III. Wm. and Mary Quar., VI, VIII, IX, XII, XVII. Va. Co. Records, I, II.

Dale. Wm. and Mary Quar., XVII. Meade's Old Fam. and Churches, I. Va. Co. Records, V, VI.

Dalton. Va. Co. Records, I.

Dameron. Wm. and Mary Quar., XI. Va. Co. Records, VI.

Dandridge. Meade's Old Fam. and Churches. Richmond, Va., Standard, II. Robertson's Pocahontas' Descendants. Spotswood Gen., by Chas. Campbell. Welle's Washington Gen. Wm. and Mary Quar., V, VI, VIII, IX, XII, XIV, XVII. Va. Hist. Mag., XIV, XV. St. Peter's Par. Reg., New Kent, Va. Old King William Homes and Families, by P. N. Clarke, 1897. Va. Co. Records, V, VI.

Daniel. Goode's Va. Cousins. Hayden's Va. Gen. Page Gen., by R. C. M. Page. Richmond, Va., Standard, I, III. Va. Co. Records, I, VI. Middlesex Par. Reg., Va. St. Peter's Par. Reg., New Kent, Va. Wm. and Mary Quar., XIII.

Darnell. Va. Co. Records, I.

Darrell. Va. Hist. Mag., XVII.

Davenport. Meade's Old Fam. and Churches. Richmond, Va., Standard, II. Wm. and Mary Quar., V, VII. Va. Co. Records, I, VI. Va. Hist. Mag., VII.

Daves. A Sketch of Capt. John Daves of the N. Carolina Contl. Line and His Family History, by Graham Daves, 1892.

Davie. Hist. of N. Carolina, by J. H. Wheeler, 1851.

Davies. Wm. and Mary Quar., VIII. Va. Co. Records, II, VI.

Davis. Va. Hist. Mag., XI, XII. Gleanings of Va. History, by W. F. Boogher, 1903. Wood's Hist. of Albemarle, Va. Va. Co. Records, I, II, III, VI, VII. Middlesex Par. Reg., Va. Wm. and Mary Quar., I, VII. Chamberlayne's Bristol Par. Reg., Va. Lower Norfolk Co., Va., Antiquary. Sidelights of Maryland Hist., by Mrs. Hester D. Richardson. Warfield's Hist. of Anne Arundel and Howard Cos., Md. Genealogy of Jeff. Davis, by W. H. Whitset, 1908. Munsell's American Ancestry, VII.

Davison. Va. Co. Records, V.

Dawley. Lower Norfolk Co., Va., Antiquary.

Dawson. Wm. and Mary Quar., I, II, V, VI, VII, IX, XI. XIII. Wood's Hist. of Albemarle. Va. Co. Records, I, VI, VII.

Day. Wm. and Mary Quar., III, VII. Va. Co. Records, I.

Dean. Richmond, Va., Standard, III. Va. Co. Records, VI.

Deans. Wm. and Mary Quar., XIII.

De Butts. Wm. and Mary Quar., XIV.

Dedman. Woods-McAfee Memorial by Woods and Durett. Wood's Hist. of Albemarle Co., Va.

De Graffenreidt. Wm. and Mary Quar., X, XI, XV.

De Kraft. Richmond, Va., Standard, III.

De Neuville. Wm. and Mary Quar., VI.

Delk. Wm. and Mary Quar., XVIII.

Denbey. Va. Co. Records, VI.

Dennett. Wm. and Mary Quar., XVII.

Denny. Richmond, Va., Standard, III.

Denwood. Va. Co. Records, VI.

Derieux. Wm. and Mary Quar., XVII.

De Veaux. History of the Bulloch and Allied Families, by J. G. Bulloch, 1892.

Devoe. Richmond, Va., Standard, III.

Dibrell. Gen. of the Lewis and Kindred Families, by J. M. McAllister and Lura B. Tandy, 1906.

Dick. Wm. and Mary Quar., XVIII. Va. Co. Records, I.

Dickerson. Wood's Hist. of Albemarle, Va.

Dickie. Hist. of the Chappell, Dickie and Kindred Families of Va., by Philip E. Chappell, 1900.

Dickinson. Va. Co. Records, I, II. Crozier's Hist. of the Buckner Fam. of Va., 1907. The McGavock Fam., by Rev. R. Gray, 1903.

Dickson. Green's Kentucky Families.

Didlake. Richmond, Va., Standard, II. Middlesex Par. Reg., Va.

Dilard. Va. Co. Records, I, VI, Middlesex Par. Reg., Va.

Dilke. Va. Hist. Mag., III.

Diggs or Digges. Meade's Old Fam. and Churches. Richmond, Va., Standard, II. Southern Bivouac, 1886. Wm. and Mary Quar., I, II, III, IV, V, VI, VIII, X, XI, XII, XV, XVII. Va. Hist. Mag., XVII. Va. Co. Records, V, VI.

Dix. Richmond, Va., Standard, II.

Dixon. Goode's Va. Cousins. Richmond, Va., Standard, III. Wm. and Mary Quar., I, III, X, XIX. Va. Co. Records, I. Rootes Fam. of Va., by W. C. Torrence, 1906.

Dobyns. Va. Co. Records, III.

Doddridge. Hayden's Va. Gen.

Dodman. Wm. and Mary Quar., IV, VII.

Dodson. Middlesex, Va., Par. Reg. Va. Co. Records, VI.

Dolby. Va. Co. Records, IV, VI.

Dollins. Wood's Hist. of Albemarle.

Donaldson. Va. Co. Records, VI.

Donithan. Wm. and Mary Quar., XVI.

Doodes. Va. Co. Records, V.

Dormer. Va. Co. Records, V.

Dorsey. Warfield's Hist. of Anne Arundel and Howard Cos., Md. MSS. Ped. Genealogical Assn.

Doswell. Wm. and Mary Quar., VIII.

Doudge. Lower Norfolk Co., Va., Antiquary.

Doughty. Va. Hist. Mag., V.

Douglas. Richmond, Va., Standard, III. Johnston's Old Va. Clerks. Wm. and Mary Quar., VIII. Va. Co. Records, V, VI. Meade's Old Fam. and Churches. Robertson's Pocahontas' Descendants. Wood's Hist. of Albemarle. The Family of Douglas of Garallan, Va. (Chart), by W. H. Abbott, 1894. Hist. of the Bulloch and Allied Families, by J. G. Bulloch, 1892.

Douthat. Richmond, Va., Standard, III.

Dowell. Wood's Hist. of Albemarle, Va.

Dowman. Hayden's Va. Gen. Va. Hist. Mag., VII. Wm. and Mary Quar., XVIII.

Dozier. Va. Co. Records, VI.

Drake. St. Peter's Par. Reg., New Kent, Va. Rootes Family of Rosewall, Va., by W. C. Torrence, 1906. Green's Kentucky Fam.

Drew. Va. Co. Records, VI.

Driver. Wm. and Mary Quar., VII.

Drummond. Wm. and Mary Quar., VI, VII, XIV.

Drury. Va. Co. Records, VI.

Dudley. Munsell's American Ancestry, VII. Va. Co. Records, I, Vl. Middlesex, Va., Par. Reg. Wm. and Mary Quar., I. Lower Norfolk Co., Va., Antiquary. Saunder's Early Settlers of Alabama.

Duerson. Va. Co. Records, I.

Duke. Richmond, Va., Standard, III. Wm. and Mary Quar., II, IX. Wood's Hist. of Albemarle, Va. The Duke-Shepherd-Van Metre Families, by Samuel G. Smyth, 1909. Va. Co. Records, V. The Buford Family in America, by M. B. Buford, 1903. Paxton's Marshall Family.

Dulany. Warfield's Hist. of Anne Arundel and Howard Cos., Md. MSS. Ped. of Genealogical Assn. Meade's Old Fam. and Churches

Dunbar. Slaughter's Hist. of St. Mark's Par., Va.

Duncanson. Va. Co. Records, I.

Duncombe. Va. Co. Records, V.

Dunkum. Wood's Hist. of Albemarle Co., Va.

Dunlop. Wm. and Mary Quar., VI, VII.

Dunn. Wm. and Mary Quar., IV. Saunder's Early Settlers of Alabama. Va. Co. Records, VI.

Dunscomb. Wm. and Mary Quar., VIII.

Dunster. Va. Hist. Mag., VI. Wm. and Mary Quar., VII.

Dunton. Va. Co. Records, VI, VII.

Dunwody. Hist. of the Bulloch and Allied Families, by J. G. Bulloch.

Dupuy. Goode's Va. Cousins. Meade's Old Fam. and Churches. Va. Hist. Collections, V. Bartholomew Dupuy and His Descendants, by Rev. B. H. Dupuy, 1908.

Durett. Va. Co. Records, I. Wood's Hist. of Albemarle, Va.

Duvall. Warfield's Hist. of Anne Arundel and Howard Cos., Md. Va. Co. Records, I. Wm. and Mary Quar., VIII. MSS. Ped. Genealogical Assn.

Dinwiddie. Dinwiddie Papers, Va. Hist. Society. Wm. and Mary
Quar., XVI, XVIII.

Dyer. Wood's Hist. of Albemarle, Va. Va. Co. Records, I, VI.
Lower Norfolk Co., Va., Antiquary. The Descendants of Saml.
Dyer of Albemarle, Va., by Charlotte P. Price (Chart), 1906.

Dykes. Wm. and Mary Quar., V.

Dyson. Slaughter's Hist. of Bristol Par., Va., 1879.

Eader. Richmond, Va., Standard, III.

Eades. Wood's Hist. of Albemarle, Va.

Earle. Munsell's American Ancestry, VII. Habersham Hist. Coll. of
Ga., II, 1902.

Early. Hist. of the Early Family in U. S., by Samuel S. Early, 1896.
Wood's Hist. of Albemarle, Va.

Eason. Rootes Fam. of Rosewall, Va., by W. C. Torrence, 1906.

Eaton. Va. Hist. Mag., V. Goodwyn's Hist. of Bruton Church, Va.
Lower Norfolk, Va., Antiquary. Col. Wm. Eaton of Granville
Co., N. C., in Davidson Coll. Mag., 1899.

Edlow. Wm. and Mary Quar., VI, VII, VIII, XV, XVI, XVIII.
Va. Hist. Mag., V.

Edmonds. Va. Co. Records, VI, VII. Lower Norfolk Co., Va.,
Antiquary.

Edmondson. Va. Co. Records, VI.

Edmunds. Meade's Old Fam. and Churches. Slaughter's Hist. of
St. Mark's Par., Va. Va. Co. Records, VI.

Edrington. Munsell's American Ancestry, VII.

Edwards. Hayden's Va. Gen. Meade's Old Fam. and Churches. Va.
Hist. Mag., V, XV. Wm. and Mary Quar., VIII, XV. John-
ston's Old Va. Clerks. Va. Co. Records, I, II, V, VI, VII.
Lower Norfolk Co., Va., Antiquary. Paxton's Marshall Family.
The Edwards and Todd Families, by Geo. H. Edwards, 1894.

Eggleston. Meade's Old Fam. and Churches.

Eldridge. Meade's Old Fam. and Churches. Richmond, Va., Standard, II. Robertson's Pocahontas' Descendants. Johnston's Old
Va. Clerks.

Ellegood. Wm. and Mary Quar., XIII. Va. Co. Records, VI.

Ellett. Johnston's Old Va. Clerks. Old King William Homes and
Families, by P. N. Clarke, 1897.

Ellicott. The Thomas Book, by L. B. Thomas, 1896.

Elliott. Middlesex Par. Reg., Va. Wm. and Mary Quar., I, II, X,
XVI, XVII. Saunder's Early Settlers of Alabama. Va. Co.
Records, II, VI. The Bulloch and Allied Families, by J. G.
Bulloch.

Ellis. Meade's Old Fam. and Churches. Wm. and Mary Quar., X.
Va. Hist. Mag., XV. Va. Co. Records, I, II, III, VI. Ellis
Family of Va. (Privately Printed), Richmond, 1907.

Ellyson. Wm. and Mary Quar., VI, X, XI, XIV, XVI.

Eltonhead. Neill's Va. Carolorum.

Embry. Meade's Old Fam. and Churches.

Emperor. Lower Norfolk Co., Va., Antiquary.

Emson. Wm. and Mary Quar., VII.

English. Wm. and Mary Quar., VII. Va. Co. Records, V, VI, VII.

Ennalls. Wm. and Mary Quar., II, IV. MSS. Ped. of Genealogical Assn.

Eppes. Meade's Old Fam. and Churches. Page Family, by R. C. M. Page, 1883. Richmond, Va., Standard, II, III. Slaughter's Hist. of Bristol Par., Va. Wm. and Mary Quar., II, V, VIII. Va. Hist. Mag., III, VII. Chamberlayne's Bristol Par. Reg., Va. Va. Co. Records, V, VI, VII. MSS. Ped. of Genealogical Assn.

Eskridge. Va. Hist. Mag., VII, VIII, IX, X. Wm. and Mary Quar., IX. MSS. Ped. of Genealogical Assn.

Estes. Genealogies of the Lewis and Kindred Families, by J. McAllister and L. B. Tandy, 1906. Va. Co. Records, I, VI.

Etheredge. Lower Norfolk Co., Va., Antiquary.

Eubank. Wood's Hist. of Albemarle, Va.

Eustace. Hayden's Va. Gen. Wm. and Mary Quar., XI.

Evans. Va. Co. Records, II, VI, VII. Wm. and Mary Quar., VII. Nathl. Evans of So. Carolina and His Descendants, by J. D. Evans, N. P., N. D.

Evelyn. Va. Hist. Mag., IX. Wm. and Mary Quar., X. Va. Co. Records, V. The Evelyns in America, by G. D. Scull, Oxford, Eng., 1881.

Everard. Meade's Old Fam. and Churches. Goodwyn's Hist. of Bruton Church, Va. Wm. and Mary Quar., IX, XIII. Sir Richard Everard of No. Carolina, and His Descendants in Va., by M. DeL. Haywood, 1897.

Everett. Crawford of Va., by R. L. Crawford, 1883. Richmond, Va., Standard, IV. Wood's Hist. of Albemarle, Va.

Eversfield. The Bowies and Their Kin, by W. W. Bowie, 1899. MSS. Ped. of the Genealogical Assn.

Ewell. Hayden's Va. Gen. Wm. and Mary Quar., IV. Lower Norfolk Co., Va., Antiquary.

Ewing. Va. Hist. Mag., IX.

Exum. Wm. and Mary Quar., VII.

Eyre. Meade's Old Fam. and Churches. Va. Co. Records, VI.

Fagg. Wood's Hist. of Albemarle Co., Va.

Fairfax. The Fairfax Family in England and America, by E. D. Neill, 1868. Goode's Va. Cousins. The Lindsays of America, by Margaret I. Lindsay, 1889. Meade's Old Fam. and Churches. Richmond, Va., Standard, IV. The Thomas Book, by L. B. Thomas. Wm. and Mary Quar., II, VII, XIII, XVIII. Va. Co. Records, V. Lee of Virginia, by E. J. Lee, 1895.

Farish. Wood's Hist. of Albemarle, Va. Va. Co. Records, I.

Farley. Oliver's Carter Tree. Meade's Old Fam. and Churches. Va. Hist. Mag., IX. Richmond Standard, II. Wm. and Mary Quar., III.

Farrar. Neill's Va. Carolorum. Southern Bivouac, 1886. Va. Hist. Mag., I, III, VII, VIII, IX, X. Richmond, Va., Standard. Some Va. Families, by H. M. McIlhany, 1903. Wood's Hist. of Albemarle, Va. Va. Co. Records, V, VI, VII.

Farmer. Va. Co. Records, II.

Farrell. Va. Hist. Mag., XI. Wm. and Mary Quar., IV.

Farrow. Crozier's Hist. of the Buckners of Va., 1907.

Faulcon. Va. Hist. Mag., V.

Faulconer. Va. Co. Records, I.

Fauntleroy. Meade's Old Fam. and Churches, II. Jones Genealogy of Va., by L. H. Jones, 1891. Va. Co. Records, I, IV. Wm. and Mary Quar., II. Descendants of Mordecai Cooke of Va., by W. C. Stubbs, 1896. Wallace's Historical Magazine, July, 1891. Of Sceptred Race, by Annah R. Watson, 1910. MSS. Ped. of Genealogical Assn.

Fauquier. Wm. and Mary Quar., VIII, XVI. Goodwyn's Hist. of Bruton Church, Va.

Faure. Va. Hist. Collections, V. Va. Co. Records, VI, VII, VIII.

Fawdon. Wm. and Mary Quar., VII.

Fearn. Lewis and Kindred Families, by McAllister and Tandy, 1906.

Feild. Goode's Va. Cousins. Slaughter's Hist. of Bristol Par. Chamberlayne's Bristol Par. Reg., Va.

Feilding. Va. Co. Records, V.

Felgate. Va. Hist. Mag., II. Wm. and Mary Quar., I.

Fentress. Lower Norfolk Co., Va., Antiquary.

Ferguson. Va. Co. Records, II. Robertson's Pocahontas' Descendants. St. Peter's Par. Reg., New Kent, Va.

Fern. Va. Hist. Mag., VI.

Ferrar. Neill's Va. Carolorum.

Ficklin. Slaughter's Hist. of St. Mark's Par. Wood's Hist. of Albemarle.

Field. Meade's Old Fam. and Churches. Slaughter's St. Mark's Par. Green's Hist. of Culpeper Co., Va. Wood's Hist. of Albemarle. Va. Hist. Mag., IV. Wm. and Mary Quar., VII. Va. Co. Records, II, VI, VII. Chamberlayne's Bristol Par. Register.

Fielding. Va. Hist. Mag., XI, XII. Wm. and Mary Quar., IX, XI, XVIII.

Filmer. Va. Co. Records, V.

Finch. St. Peter's Par. Reg., New Kent, Va. Wm. and Mary Quar., XVI.

Finney. Va. Co. Records, IV.

Fisher. Va. Co. Records, II, VI, VII. Richmond, Va., Standard, II. Some Va. Families, by H. M. McIlhany, 1903. Wheeler's History of N. Carolina.

Fitch. Wood's Hist. of Albemarle Co., Va.

Fitts. Genealogy of the Fitts or Fitz Family in America, by J. H. Fitts, 1897.

Fitzhugh. Carter Family Tree, by Oliver. Meade's Old Fam. and Churches. Richmond, Va., Standard, II, III. Va. Hist. Mag., I, II, VII, VIII, IX. Welle's Washington Genealogy. The Thomas Book, by L. B. Thomas. Va. Co. Records, I, IV, VI, VII. Wm. and Mary Quar., I, II, III. Descendants of Mordecai Cooke, Va., by W. C. Stubbs. Lee of Va., by E. J. Lee, 1895.

Fleet. Va. Hist. Mag., II, V. Va. Co. Records, III, IV, V, VI.

Fleming. The Bolling Fam. in England and Va., by Robert Bolling, 1868. Goode's Va. Cousins. Meade's Old Fam. and Churches. Richmond, Va., Standard, II, IV. Robertson's Pocahontas' Descendants. Va. Hist. Mag., X. Wm. and Mary Quar., I, VI, XII. Va. Co. Records, II, VI, VII. Paxton's Marshall Family.

Fletcher. Va. Co. Records, VI, VII.

Flint. Saunder's Early Settlers of Alabama, 1899. Va. Co. Records, VI, VII.

Flood. Wm. and Mary Quar., VII, XI, XIII, XVI. Va. Co. Records, VI, VII.

Flournoy. Richmond, Va., Standard, I, III. Va. Hist. Mag., II, III, IV. Wm. and Mary Quar., XVI. Crozier's Hist. of the Buckners of Va., 1907. Va. Co. Records, V.

Flower. Va. Hist. Mag., XI. Wm. and Mary Quar., III. Va. Co. Records, V.

Floyd. Oliver's Carter Family Tree. Richmond, Va., Standard, II. Habersham Hist. Coll. of Ga., I. Va. Hist. Mag., VII. Va. Co. Records, VI, VII.

Folliott. Va. Co. Records, V. Wm. and Mary Quar., I, IV, VII. Va. Hist. Mag., XVI.

Fontaine. Meade's Old Fam. and Churches. Slaughter's Fry Gen. Slaughter's Hist. of St. Mark's Par. Welle's Washington Gen. Va. Hist. Collections, V. Va. Hist. Mag., VI. Wm. and Mary Quar., I, V, VI. Va. Co. Records, V. Green's Kentucky Families.

Foote. Wm. and Mary Quar., XI. Va. Hist. Mag., II, VII. Va. Co. Records, V.

Forbes. St. Peter's Par. Reg., New Kent, Va.

Ford. Va. Co. Records, II, VI, VII, VIII.

Forman. The Descendants of Robert Forman of Md., by Miss A. S. Dandridge, 1903. Paxton's Marshall Family.

Forney. Wheeler's Hist. of N. Carolina.

Forrest. Richmond, Va., Standard, III.

Forsyth. Munsell's American Ancestry, VII. Richmond Standard, III. Woods-McAfee Memorial, by Woods and Durett, 1905. Warfield's Founders of Anne Arundel and Howard Cos., Md.

Fort. Memoirs of the Fort and Fannin Families, by Kate H. Fort, 1903.

Fossaker. Va. Hist. Mag., XV.

Foster. Va. Co. Records, I, II, VI, VII, VIII. St. Peter's Par. Reg., New Kent, Va. Wm. and Mary Quar., II. Keith's Harrison Ancestry. Saunder's Early Settlers of Alabama, 1899.

Foulke. Hayden's Va. Gen.

Foushee. Va. Hist. Mag., VII.

Fowke. Hayden's Va. Gen. Meade's Old Fam. and Churches. Wm. and Mary Quar., IV. Va. Co. Records, V.

Fowler. Annals of the Fowler Family of Va., N. C., S. C., Tenn., Ky., Ala., Miss., Cal., and Texas, by Mrs. Glenn D. F. Arthur, 1901. Va. Co. Records, II, VI, VII.

Fox. Hayden's Va. Gen. Richmond Standard, III. Va. Hist. Mag., VIII. Wm. and Mary Quar., III, VIII, XVII. Va. Co. Records, I, II, V, VI, VII.

Francis. Hist. of Old Kent, Md., by G. A. Hanson, 1876.

Francisco. Peter Francisco, Soldier of the Revolution, by Miss N. B. Winston, 1893. Wm. and Mary Quar., XIII, XIV.

Franklin. Hayden's Va. Gen. Va. Co. Records, I, II.

Fraser. So. Carolina Hist. and Genl. Mag., V.

Frasher. Va. Co. Records, I.

Frazier. Richmond Standard, IV. Va. Co. Records, I.

Freeman. Wm. and Mary Quar., II. Va. Co. Records, II, VI, VII.

Fremont. Richmond, Va., Standard, II.

French. Va. Co. Records, I, VI, VII. Middlesex Par. Reg., Va. Wm. and Mary Quar., XII.

Freshwater. Va. Co. Records, VI.

Fretwell. Wood's Hist. of Albemarle Co., Va.

Frisby. Hanson's Hist. of Old Kent, Md. The Thomas Family of Md., by L. B. Thomas.

Frogg. Green's Kentucky Families.

Fry. Slaughter's Fry Gen., 1880. Goode's Va. Cousins. Meade's Old Fam. and Churches. Richmond, Va., Standard, III, Slaughter's Hist. of St. Mark's Par., Va. Wm. and Mary Quar., II, X, XVII Green's Hist. of Culpeper Co., Va. Wood's Hist. of Albemarle, Va. Paxton's Marshall Family. Saunder's Early Settlers of Alabama. Va. Co. Records, II.

Fulgham. Wm. and Mary Quar., VII. Va. Co. Records, VI.

Fulkerson. The Gentry Family in America, by Richard Gentry, 1909

Fulton. Richmond Standard, III. Va. Hist. Mag., X.

Furman. The So. Carolina Furmans as Educators, by McD. Furman, 1897.

Gaines. Goode's Va. Cousins. Meade's Old Fam. and Churches. Richmond Standard, III. Slaughter's Hist. of St. Mark's Par., Va. Munsell's American Ancestry, VII. Va. Co. Records, I, VI, VII. Crozier's Buckner Family of Va., 1907. Wm. and Mary Quar., V.

Gaither. Warfield's Founders of Anne Arundel and Howard Cos., Md.

Gale. Va. Co. Records, I.

Gallaher. MSS. Ped. of the Genealogical Assn.

Galloway. The Thomas Book, by L. B. Thomas, 1896.

Galt. Richmond Standard, III. Wm. and Mary Quar., I, VIII, IX. Goodwyn's Hist. of Bruton Church, Va.

Gamble. Goode's Va. Cousins. Richmond Standard, II.

Gambrill. Warfield's Hist. of Anne Arundel and Howard Cos., Md.

Gantt. Wood's Hist. of Albemarle, Va. Hist. of the Hay Family of So. Carolina, by C. J. Colcock, 1908.

Gardner. Va. Co. Records, I, VI, VII. Middlesex, Va., Par. Reg. Lee of Va., by E. J. Lee, 1895. Letters and Times of the Tylers, by L. G. Tyler, 1897.

Garland. Goode's Va. Cousins. Meade's Old Fam. and Churches. Wm. and Mary Quar., VII. Va. Co. Records, VI.

Garlick. Wm. and Mary Quar., IV, XVI. Va. Co. Records, I, V.

Garner. Va. Co. Records, I.

Garnett. Meade's Old Fam. and Churches. Richmond Standard, III. Slaughter's Hist. of St. Mark's Par., Va. Green's Hist. of Culpeper, Va. Va. Co. Records, I.

Garr. Genealogy of John Garr and His Descendants, by J. W. and J. C. Garr, 1894.

Garrard. Gov. Garrard of Kentucky and His Descendants, by Anna R. des Cognets, 1898.

Garrett. Warfield's Founders of Anne Arundel and Howard Cos., Md. Va. Co. Records, I, VI. Johnston's Old Va. Clerks. Wood's Hist. of Albemarle, Va. Middlesex, Va., Par. Reg. Wm. and Mary Quar., V. Goodwyn's Hist. of Bruton Church, Va. Chamberlayne's Bristol Par. Reg., Va.

Garrison. Lower Norfolk, Va., Antiquary.

Garth. Wood's Hist. of Albemarle, Va.

Garton. Va. Co. Records, I.

Gary. Nathl. Evans of So. Carolina and His Descendants, by James D. Evans.

Gascoyne. Va. Co. Records, VI.

Gaskins. Hayden's Va. Gen. Wm. and Mary Quar., I, V, XI. Va. Hist. Mag., V. Notes on the Gaskins Family (Sheet), by Thos. L. Broun, 1906.

Gassaway. Founders of Anne Arundel and Howard Cos., Md.

Gaston. Wheeler's Hist. of N. Carolina. Wheeler's Eminent North Carolinians, 1884.

Gatewood. Richmond Standard, III. Welle's Washington Genealogy. Va. Co. Records, I, II.

Gay. Meade's Old Fam. and Churches. Robertson's Pocahontas' Descendants.

Gentry. Wood's Hist. of Albemarle, Va. Gentry Family of Va., by Richard Gentry, 1909.

George. Middlesex, Va., Par. Reg. Wm. and Mary Quar., VII. The Thomas Book, by L. B. Thomas. Va. Co. Records, VI.

Gerrard. Wm. and Mary Quar., IV, V.

Gholson. Meade's Old Fam. and Churches. Richmond Standard, II. Va. Co. Records, I. Saunder's Early Settlers of Alabama.

Gibbens. The Gibbens-Butcher Genealogy of Va., by A. F. Gibbens, 1894.

Gibbons. Wm. and Mary Quar., I.

Gibbs. Richmond Standard, III. Middlesex, Va., Par. Reg. Chamberlayne's Bristol Par. Reg.

Gibson. Peyton's Hist. of Augusta Co., Va. Richmond Standard, II. Va. Co. Records, I, II, VI. Middlesex, Va., Par. Reg. Habersham Hist. Coll. of Ga., II.

Gilbert. Sketches of the First Families of Upper Georgia, by Geo. R. Gilmer, 1855. Va. Co. Records, VI.

Giles. Crawford Family of Va., by R. L. Crawford, 1883. Va. Co. Records, VI.

Gill. Warfield's Founders of Anne Arundel and Howard Cos., Md. Wm. and Mary Quar., VIII. Va. Hist. Mag., VI. Chamberlayne's Bristol Par. Reg.

Gillespie. Va. Co. Records, II.

Gilliam. Richmond, Va., Standard, II, III. Slaughter's Hist. of Bristol Par. St. Peter's Par. Reg., New Kent, Va. Wm. and Mary Quar., XII. Chamberlayne's Bristol Par. Reg.

Gilmer. Page Gen., by R. C. M. Page, 1883. Meade's Old Fam. and Churches. The Meriwethers and the Connections, by L. H. A. Minor, 1892. Peyton's Hist. of Augusta Co., Va. Richmond Standard, I. Wm. and Mary Quar., VI, VII, XV. Wood's Hist. of Albemarle, Va. Va. Co. Records, V.

Gilpin. The Thomas Book, by L. B. Thomas, 1896.

Gissage. Wm. and Mary Quar., X, XI.

Gist. Va. Hist. Mag., VII. Va. Co. Records, II. Paxton's Marshall Gen.

Glascock. Wm. and Mary Quar., XVII. Va. Hist. Mag., VII.

Glass. Wm. and Mary Quar., VIII. Va. Co. Records, VI.

Glasgow. The Thomas Book, by L. B. Thomas, 1896.

Glassell. Hayden's Va. Gen. Slaughter's Hist. of St. Mark's Par. Va. Hist. Mag., X. Green's Hist. of Culpeper Co., Va. Va. Co. Records, I.

Glenn. The Bulloch and Allied Families, by J. G. Bulloch, 1892. St. Peter's Par. Reg., New Kent., Va.

Glover. Va. Hist. Mag., XI. Va. Co. Records, VI.

Godbold. Nathaniel Evans of So. Carolina and His Descendants, by J. D. Evans.

Godfrey. Va. Co. Records, VI. Lower Norfolk Co., Va., Antiquary.

Godwin. Va. Hist. Mag., V, VI, XVII. Wm. and Mary Quar., VII.

Goff. Va. Co. Records, VI.

Goldsborough. Hanson's Hist. of Old Kent, Md. Warfield's Hist. of Anne Arundel and Howard Cos., Md.

Gooch. Wm. and Mary Quar., II, V, VI. Wood's Hist. of Albemarle. Va. Co. Records, V. Goodwyn's Hist. of Bruton Church, Va.

Goode. Va. Cousins, A Study of the Ancestry of John Goode of Whitby and Va., by G. B. Goode, 1887. Va. Co. Records, II. Saunder's Early Settlers of Alabama.

Goodloe. Va. Co. Records, I. Middlesex, Va., Par. Reg.

Goodman. Wood's Hist. of Albemarle, Va.

Goodrich. Va. Co. Records, II, VI. Wm. and Mary Quar., II, VII, XVI. Va. Hist. Mag., XV.

Goodwin. Wm. and Mary Quar., Supplementary Vol. for 1897. Va. Co. Records, I, II, V. Middlesex, Va., Par. Reg. Goodwyn's Hist. of Bruton Church, Va. St. Peter's Par. Reg., New Kent, Va. Chamberlayne's Bristol Par. Reg. Meade's Old Fam. and Churches.

Gookin. Richmond Standard, IV. Wm. and Mary Quar., IX. Va. Hist. Mag., V. Va. Co. Records, V. New Eng. Hist. and Genl. Reg., I, II.

Goolsby. Wood's Hist. of Albemarle, Va.

Goosley. Wm. and Mary Quar., I, VII.

Gordan. Richmond, Va., Critic, 1888.

Gordon. Goode's Va. Cousins. Hayden's Va. Gen. Richmond Standard, III. Robertson's Pocahontas' Descendants. Slaughter's Bristol Par. Wm. and Mary Quar., XI. Va. Hist. Mag., X. Wood's Hist. of Albemarle, Va. Va. Co. Records, I, II, V, VI. Middlesex, Va., Par. Reg. Munsell's American Ancestry, VII. Hist. of Orange Co., Va., by W. W. Scott, 1907. Green's Kentucky Families. MSS. Ped. of Genealogical Assn.

Goring. Wm. and Mary Quar., VII.

Gorsuch. MSS. Ped. of Genealogical Assn. Va. Hist. Mag., III, XVII.

Gosnold. Va. Hist. Mag., XIV.

Goss. Wood's Hist. of Albemarle, Va.

Gough. Va. Co. Records, VI.

Gower. Va. Hist. Mag., VII, XVII. Va. Co. Records, VI.

Graham. Hayden's Va. Gen. Richmond, Va., Standard, III. Va. Co. Records, II, V, VI. Roger Jones of Va., and His Descendants, by L. H. Jones, 1891. Wm. and Mary Quar., XVII.

Granger. Va. Co. Records, VI.

Grant. Munsell's American Ancestry, VII. Warfield's Hist. of Anne Arundel and Howard Cos., Md.

Grason. Warfield's Hist. of Anne Arundel and Howard Cos., Md.

Grasty. Va. Co. Records, I.

Grattan. Gilmer's Georgians, 1855.

Graves. Hayden's Va. Gen. Meade's Old Fam. and Churches. Wm. and Mary Quar., II, III, XII. Va. Co. Records, I, VI.

Gray. Richmond, Va., Standard, III. Slaughter's Hist. of St. Mark's Par. Va. Hist. Mag., III, V, X, XI. Wm. and Mary Quar., XII. Rootes Fam. of Va., by W. C. Torrence, 1906. Va. Co. Records, II, V, VI.

Grayson. Meade's Old Fam. and Churches. Wood's Hist of Albemarle. Va. Co. Records, I.

Green. Goode's Va. Cousins. Hayden's Va. Gen. Meade's Old Fam. and Churches. Richmond Standard, II, III. Slaughter's Fry Gen. Slaughter's Hist. of St. Mark's Par. Green's Hist. of Culpeper Co., Va. Va. Hist. Mag., VIII, IX, X. Va. Co. Records, I, II, VI. Va. Hist. Collections, V. St. Peter's Par. Reg., New Kent, Va. Chamberlayne's Bristol Par. Reg. Paxton's Marshall Family.

Greenberry. Warfield's Hist. of Anne Arundel and Howard Cos., Md.

Greene. Habersham Hist. Coll. of Ga., I.

Greenhow. Richmond Standard II. Wm. and Mary Quar., VII, XVII.

Greenlee. Paxton's Marshall Family.

Greenway. Meade's Old Fam. and Churches.

Greenwood. Munsell's American Ancestry, VII. Middlesex Par. Reg.

Gregg. Nathaniel Evans of So. Carolina and His Descendants, by J. D. Evans.

Gregory. Richmond Standard, II. Slaughter's Fry Gen. Va. Hist. Mag., V, XV, XVI. Va. Co. Records, I, VI. Wm. and Mary Quar., XI, XVI. Chamberlayne's Bristol Par. Reg.

Grendon. Va. Hist. Mag., I, XIV.

Gresham. Goode's Va. Cousins. Middlesex Par. Reg. Va. Co. Records, VI.

Griffin. Hayden's Va. Gen. Meade's Old Fam. and Churches. Richmond Standard, I, III. Va. Hist. Mag., I, V, VII. Goodwyn's Hist. of Bruton Church, Va. Wm. and Mary Quar., VII. Va. Co. Records, II, V, VI.

Griffith. Warfield's Hist. of Anne Arundel and Howard Cos., Md. The Thomas Family of Md., by L. B. Thomas. Va. Co. Records, VI.

Grigsby. Wm. and Mary Quar., IX. Gen. of the Grigsby Family, by H. H. McCormick, 1905 (Orig. Pub.), by W. H. Grigsby, 1878. Grigsby MSS., property of the Genealogical Assn.

Grimes. Va. Co. Records, VI.

Grinnan. Hayden's Va. Gen. Green's Hist. of Culpeper Co., Va.

Grove. Wm. and Mary Quar., VII.

Grymes. Oliver's Carter Family Tree. Meade's Old Fam. and Churches. Page of Va., by R. C. M. Page, 1883. Richmond Standard, III. Va.' Hist. Mag., V, VIII. Wm. and Mary Quar., V, VI. Va. Co. Records, I, II, V, VI. Middlesex Par. Reg. Rootes Fam. of Va., by W. C. Torrence, 1906. Lee of Va., by E. J. Lee, 1895. Richmond, Va., Critic, 18th Aug., 1889.

Guerrant. Wm. and Mary Quar., IX, XI.

Gurley. Wm. and Mary Quar., VIII.

Guthrie. Records of the Guthries of Pa., Conn., and Va., by H. N. and E. G. Dunn, 1898. Middlesex Par. Reg. Va. Co. Records, VI.

Guy. Va. Co. Records, VI.

Gwathmey. Richmond Standard, II, III, IV. Welle's Washington Gen.

Gwatkin. Wm. and Mary Quar., V.

Gwinnett. Habersham Hist. Coll. of Ga., I. Habersham Fam., by J. G. Bulloch.

Gwynn. Hayden's Va. Gen. Wm. and Mary Quar., XVIII. Va. Co. Records, I, VI.

Habersham. Habersham Hist. Coll. of Ga., I.

Hack. Hayden's Va. Gen. Va. Hist. Mag., V.

Hackley. Meade's Old Fam. and Churches. Va. Co. Records, I.

Hackney. Va. Co. Records, I. Middlesex Par. Reg.

Haggard. The Gentry Family in Va., by Richard Gentry, 1909. Munsell's American Ancestry, VII.

Hairston. Meade's Old Fam. and Churches.

Haley. Va. Co. Records, I.

Hall. Warfield's Hist. of Anne Arundel and Howard Cos., Md. Hanson's Hist. of Old Kent, Md. Oliver's Carter Tree. Welle's Washington Gen. Va. Co. Records, I, II, VI. Wm. and Mary Quar., IV, VII, IX, XIII. Chamberlayne's Bristol Par. Reg. Lower Norfolk, Va., Antiquary. The Families of Lyman Hall of Georgia, by T. P. Hall, 1886.

Hallam. Va. Hist. Mag., XIII. Wm. and Mary Quar., VIII.

Halliman. Wm. and Mary Quar., VII.

Halsey. Slaughter's Hist. of St. Mark's Par., Va.

Hamilton. Slaughter's Hist. of St. Mark's Par., Va. Habersham Hist. Coll. of Ga., I. Grigsby Fam., by H. H. McCormick, 1905. Va. Co. Records, II, VI.

Hamlin. Chamberlayne's Bristol Par. Reg. Wm. and Mary Quar., XI.

Hammond. Warfield's Hist. of Anne Arundel and Howard Cos., Md. Va. Co. Records, VI.

Hamner. Wood's Hist. of Albemarle Co., Va.

Hamor. Neill's Va. Carolorum. Wm. and Mary Quar., X.

Hampton. Richmond Standard, II. Habersham Hist. Coll. of Ga., I.

Hancock. Wood's Hist. of Albemarle, Va. Va. Co. Records, VI.

Handford. Va. Hist. Mag., VIII, XVI.

Hanger. Peyton's Hist. of Augusta Co., Va.

Hanna. Va. Hist. Mag., XVI.

Hansford. Meade's Old Fam. and Churches. Goodwyn's Hist. of Bruton Church, Va. Va. Co. Records, V.

Hanson. Lee of Va., by E. J. Lee, 1895. Hanson's Hist. of Old Kent, Md.

Harbeson. Richmond Standard, III. Paxton's Marshall Family. Green's Kentucky Families.

Hardaway. Thomas Hardaway of Chesterfield Co., Va., and His Descendants, by Sarah D. Hubert, 1906. Meade's Old Fam. and Churches. Chamberlayne's Bristol Par. Reg.

Harden. Munsell's American Ancestry, VII. Wood's Hist. of Albemarle. Collin's Hist. of Kentucky, 1847. Green's Kentucky Families.

Hardidge. Va. Hist. Mag., XV.

Harding. Crawford Fam. of Va., by R. J. Crawford. Richmond Standard, III, IV. Wm. and Mary Quar., VIII.

Hardwich. Wm. and Mary Quar., IV.

Hardy. Va. Hist. Mag., VIII. Wm. and Mary Quar., IV, VII. Va. Co. Records, VI.

Hardyman. Wm. and Mary Quar., V, VIII, XI. Va. Hist. Mag., VII.

Hare. Wm. and Mary Quar., VIII.

Harlan. Munsell's American Ancestry, VII.

Harleston. So. Carolina Hist. and Genl. Mag., III.

Harmanson. Va. Co. Records, VI. Wm. and Mary Quar., VII.

Harmar. Va. Co. Records, VI. Va. Hist. Mag., III. Meade's Old Fam. and Churches.

Harper. Wood's Hist. of Albemarle, Va. Va. Co. Records, VI. Wm. and Mary Quar., III.

Harris. The Descendants of Capt. Thos. Harris of Henrico, Va., by W. G. Stanard, 1893. Richmond Standard, II. Robertson's Pocahontas' Descendants. Va. Hist. Mag., IV. Wood's Hist. of Albemarle. Va. Co. Records, I, II, VI. St. Peter's Par. Reg., New Kent., Va. Wm. and Mary Quar., VII. Chamberlayne's Bristol Par. Reg. The Gentry Fam. in Va., by Richard Gentry, 1909. Thomas Family of Md., by L. B. Thomas. Edward Harris and His Ancestors, by W. P. Johnston, 1899.

Harrison. Campbell's Hist. of Va. Oliver's Carter Family Tree. Goode's Va. Cousins. Keith's Harrison Ancestry, 1893. Hayden's Va. Gen. Sketches of Lynchburg, by Mrs. Julia M. Cabell, 1858. Meade's Old Fam. and Churches. Page Gen., by R. C. M. Page, 1883. Richmond, Va., Critic, 28th Dec., 1888. Robertson's Pocahontas' Descendants. Slaughter's Hist. of Bristol Par. Wm. and Mary Quar., I, IV, VII, VIII, X, XVIII. Va. Hist. Mag., II, III, VI, VII, X. Gleanings of Va. History, by W. F. Boogher, 1903. Wood's Hist. of Albemarle. Va. Co. Records, I, II, V, VI, VII. Goodwyn's Hist. of Bruton Church. Chamberlayne's Bristol Par. Reg. The Lower Norfolk Co. Antiquary. The Harrisons of Va., in Notes and Queries, 3d Series, Vol. III, Edited by W. H. Egle, 1896.

Harry. Gen. of the Bell Family of Md., 1894.

Hart. Wood's Hist. of Albemarle. Va. Co. Records, I, VI.

Hartwell. Va. Hist. Mag., IV. Wm. and Mary Quar., VI, VII.

Harvey. Wm. and Mary Quar., XI.

Harvie. Meade's Old Fam. and Churches. Wood's Hist. of Albemarle. Green's Kentucky Families. Paxton's Marshall Family.

Harward. Va. Co. Records, V.

Harwood. Warfield's Founders of Anne Arundel and Howard Cos., Md. Richmond Standard, II, III. Wm. and Mary Quar., I, X, XI, XIV. Va. Hist. Mag., II, VIII. Goodwyn's Hist. of Bruton Church. Va. Co. Records, V, VI.

Hatcher. Va. Hist. Mag., V. Va. Co. Records, VI.

Hawes. Crozier's Buckners of Va., 1907.

Hawkins. Meade's Old Fam. and Churches. Va. Hist. Mag., III, IV. Va. Co. Records, I, II, VI. Chamberlayne's Bristol Par. Reg. The Gentry Family in Va., by R. Gentry, 1909. Warfield's Founders of Anne Arundel and Howard Cos., Md. Green's Kentucky Families. Wheeler's Hist. of No. Carolina, 1851. Wheeler's Eminent No. Carolinians, 1884.

Hawks. Chamberlayne's Bristol Par. Reg.

Hawley. Neill's Va. Carolorum. Va. Co. Records, VI.

Haxall. Hayden's Va. Gen. Slaughter's Bristol Par. Wm. and Mary Quar., XII.

Hay. Hist. of the Hay Family of So. Carolina, by C. J. Colcock, 1908. Richmond Standard, II. Wm. and Mary Quar., III, V, VII, XV.

Hayden. Hayden's Va. Gen. Va. Co. Records, I.

Hayes. Richmond Standard, III. Va. Co. Records, VI.

Hayne. So. Car. Hist. and Genl. Mag., V.

Haynes. Meade's Old Fam. and Churches. Va. Hist. Mag., XV. Lower Norfolk Co., Va., Antiquary.

Haynie. Wm. and Mary Quar., VIII, XVIII.

Hays. Wood's Hist. of Albemarle. Wm. and Mary Quar., IX. The Descendants of John Walker of Va., by Emma S. White, 1902. Va. Co. Records, VI.

Hayward. Va. Hist. Mag., I. Wm. and Mary Quar., XI.

Haywood. Wheeler's Hist. of No. Carolina, 1851.

Head. Va. Co. Records, I.

Heale. Wm. and Mary Quar., VI, XVII.

Heard. Hist. Coll. of the Habersham Chapter, D. A. R., II, 1902.

Heath. Meade's Old Fam. and Churches. Wm. and Mary Quar., IX, XI. Va. Co. Records, I, VI. St. Peter's Par. Reg., New Kent, Va.

Heatwole. Hist. of the Heatwole Fam., by D. A. Heatwole, 1882.

Hedgman. Hayden's Va. Gen.

Helm. Green's Kentucky Families.

Henderson. Hayden's Va. Gen. Meade's Old Fam. and Churches. Richmond Standard, III. Ancestry and Descendants of Lieut. John Henderson of Greenbrier, Va., by J. L. Miller, M.D., 1902. Wood's Hist. of Albemarle. Va. Co. Records, I, II, V, VI. Wm. and Mary Quar., VIII. Wheeler's Hist. of No. Carolina. Wheeler's Eminent No. Carolinians. Richmond, Va., Critic, 9th June, 1899. Hist. of Truro Parish, Va., by Rev. Philip Slaughter.

Hening. Goode's Va. Cousins. Hayden's Va. Gen. Wood's Hist. of Albemarle.

Henley. Wm. and Mary Quar., I, V, VII. Richmond Standard, IV. Lower Norfolk Co., Antiquary. Goodwyn's Hist. of Bruton Church.

Henry. Hist. of the Henry Family, by J. F. Henry, 1900. Campbell's Hist. of Va. Goode's Va. Cousins. Hayden's Va. Gen. Richmond Standard, I, II, IV. Slaughter's Hist. of St. Mark's Par., Va. Va. Hist. Mag., V. Warfield's Hist. of Anne Arundel and Howard Cos., Md. Saunder's Early Settlers of Alabama.

Hensley. Va. Co. Records, I.

Hepbron. Hanson's Hist. of Old Kent, Md.

Herbert. Meade's Old Fam. and Churches. Richmond Standard, III. Slaughter's Hist. of Bristol Par. Wm. and Mary Quar., V, VIII, XIII. The Thomas Book, by L. B. Thomas. Va. Hist. Mag., V. Va. Co. Records, III, V. Chamberlayne's Bristol Par. Reg. Lower Norfolk Co., Antiquary.

Herndon. Va. Hist. Mag., IX, X, XI, XII. Va. Co. Records, I, II.

Heslop. Va. Co. Records, I.

Heth. Richmond Standard, II. Paxton's Marshall Family.

Hext. So. Carolina Genl. and Hist. Mag., VI.

Heyman. Va. Hist. Mag., XI. Va. Co. Records, V.

Heyward. Wm. and Mary Quar., II. Va. Co. Records, VI. Genl. Chart of Heyward of So. Carolina, by B. R. Heyward, 1896. The Colonial History of Heyward of So. Carolina, by James B. Heyward, 1907.

Heywood. Wheeler's Eminent No. Carolinians.

Hickey. Richmond, Va., Standard, II.

Hickman. Wm. and Mary Quar., III, X. Va. Co. Records, I, II. The Buford Family in America, by M. B. Buford, 1903. Jones Family of Va., by L. H. Jones, 1891.

Hicks. Meade's Old Fam. and Churches. Wm. and Mary Quar., XI.

Higginson. Wm. and Mary Quar., II, III, V, VI. Va. Hist. Mag., IV.

Hill. Meade's Old Fam. and Churches. Richmond Standard, III. Va. Hist. Mag., III, X, XI, XIV. Slaughter's Hist. of St. Mark's Par., Va. Green's Hist. of Culpeper Co., Va. Wm. and Mary Quar., I, III, IV, V, VI, VII, VIII, XVI. The Century Mag., XLI. Va. Co. Records, I, II, V, VI. Middlesex Par. Reg., Va. St. Peter's Par. Reg., New Kent, Va. Chamberlayne's Bristol Par. Reg. Hill Family of King and Queen Co., Va., by Mrs. G. C. Courtney, 1905. Wheeler's Hist. of No. Carolina. MSS. Ped. of Genealogical Assn.

Hillyer. Richmond, Va., Standard, III.

Hilton. St. Peter's Par. Reg., New Kent, Va. Richmond Standard, I.

Hinton. Wm. and Mary Quar., II. Chamberlayne's Bristol Par. Reg.

Hite. Slaughter's Hist. of St. Mark's Par. Wm. and Mary Quar., IV, X. Paxton's Marshall Family.

Hillen. MSS. Ped. of the Genealogical Assn.

Hillary. MSS. Ped. of the Genealogical Assn.

Hobbs. Chamberlayne's Bristol Par. Reg. Warfield's Founders of Anne Arundel and Howard Cos., Md.

Hobson. Richmond Standard, III. Wm. and Mary Quar., X, XI, XVII. Va. Co. Records, I. Va. Hist. Mag., IX. Habersham Hist. Coll. of Ga., II.

Hoccaday. Va. Co. Records, VI.

Hodges. Meade's Old Fam. and Churches. Goodwyn's Hist. of Bruton Church. Va. Hist. Mag., XVII. Va. Co. Records, VI. Lower Norfolk Co. Antiquary. Hanson's Hist. of Old Kent, Md.

Hodson. Va. Co. Records, VI.

Hoffman. Richmond Standard, II.

Hoge. Foote's Sketches of Va., II. MSS. Ped. of Genealogical Assn.

Hogg. Va. Co. Records, II.

Holden. Wm. and Mary Quar., V.

Holford. Va. Co. Records, V.

Holladay or Holliday. Hayden's Va. Gen. Va. Co. Records, I. Meade's Old Fam. and Churches. Hanson's Old Kent, Md.

Holland. Va. Co. Records, VI. Wm. and Mary Quar., IV.

Hollingsworth. The Joliffe Family of Va., by Wm. Joliffe, 1893. MSS. Ped. of Genealogical Assn.

Hollman. Wm. and Mary Quar., IX.

Holloway. Some Va. Families, by H. M. McIlhany, 1903. Va. Co. Records, I, VI, VII.

Holmes. Meade's Old Fam. and Churches. Wm. and Mary Quar., XVI. Hist. Coll. of Habersham Chapter of Ga., I. Va. Co. Records, I.

Holmewood. Va. Co. Records, VI.

Holt. Va. Hist. Mag., V. Goodwyn's Hist. of Bruton Church, Va. Wm. and Mary Quar., I, VII, XVII. Va. Co. Records, VI.

Hone. Va. Hist. Mag., IV. Wm. and Mary Quar., VI. Va. Co. Records, V.

Homewood. Warfield's Hist. of Anne Arundel and Howard Cos., Md.

Honeywood. Wm. and Mary Quar., III.

Hood. Chamberlayne's Bristol Par. Reg. Warfield's Hist. of Anne Arundel and Howard Cos., Md.

Hooe. Hayden's Va. Gen. Meade's Old Fam. and Churches. Richmond Standard, III. De Bows Review, XXIX. Va. Hist. Mag., IV, XII. Wm. and Mary Quar., II, VII. Va. Co. Records, IV.

Hooke. Va. Hist. Mag., III. Va. Co. Records, V.

Hope. Wm. and Mary Quar., VIII.

Hopgood. Va. Co. Records, VI, VII.

Hopkins. Meade's Old Fam. and Churches. Wood's Hist. of Albemarle. St. Peter's Par. Reg., New Kent, Va., Warfield's Hist. of Anne Arundel and Howard Cos., Md. The Thomas Book, by L. B. Thomas, 1896. Saunder's Early Settlers of Alabama. Va. Co. Records, VI.

Hord. Genealogy of the Hord Family, by Rev. A. H. Hord, 1898. Supplement to Genealogy of the Hord Family, by Rev. A. H. Hord, 1903. Va. Co. Records, I. Buckners of Va., by Wm. A. Crozier, 1907.

Horner. Hayden's Va. Gen. Hist. of the Blair, Banister and Braxton Families, by F. Horner, M.D., 1898.

Hornsby. Some Notable Families of America, by Annah R. Watson, 1898.

Horsley. Va. Co. Records, VI.

Horsmanden. Wm. and Mary Quar., IX. Va. Hist. Mag., XV.

Horton. Va. Co. Records, VI.

Horwitz. MSS. Ped. of the Genealogical Assn.

Hoskins. Jones Gen., by L. H. Jones, 1891.

Hough. Va. Hist. Mag., XIII. Va. Co. Records, VI, VII.

House. Va. Co. Records, II.

Houston. The Houston Family of Va., by Rev. S. R. Houston, 1882. Va. Co. Records, I.

Howard. Meade's Old Fam. and Churches. Richmond Standard, II, III. Wm. and Mary Quar., I, II, IV, VI, VII, VIII, IX, X. Middlesex, Va., Par. Reg. Va. Co. Records, II, VI. Warfield's Hist. of Anne Arundel and Howard Cos., Md. The Thomas Book, by L. B. Thomas, 1896. Hanson's Old Kent, Md. MSS. Ped. of the Genealogical Assn.

Howe. Va. Hist. Mag., II. Va. Co. Records, VI.

Howell. St. Peter's Par. Reg., New Kent, Va. Va. Co. Records, V, VI.

Howson. Va. Hist. Mag., IV.

Hubard or Hubbard. Meade's Old Fam. and Churches. Wm. and Mary Quar., I, III, IV, V, VI, XVIII. Va. Co. Records, I, V, VI. St. Peter's Par. Reg., New Kent, Va. Goodwyn's Hist. of Bruton Church, Va.

Huddleston. Va. Co. Records, I.

Hudson. Wood's Hist. of Albemarle. Middlesex, Va., Par. Reg. Wm. and Mary Quar., V. Chamberlayne's Bristol Par. Reg. Va. Co. Records, II, VI, VII. Habersham Hist. Coll. of Ga., II.

Hughes. Minor's Meriwether Gen. Richmond Standard, I, III. Va. Hist. Mag., V. Wood's Hist. of Albemarle. Va. Co. Records, I, II, VI, VII. Middlesex, Va., Par. Reg. St. Peter's Par. Reg., New Kent, Va.

Hulett. Va. Co. Records, I, VI, VII.

Hull. Richmond Standard, III. Va. Co. Records, VI.

Hume. Wm. and Mary Quar., VI, VIII, XIII. Va. Co. Records, I, V. History of the Hume Family, published by the Hume Genl. Assn., 1903.

Humphreys. Va. Co. Records, I, II, VI. Middlesex, Va., Par. Reg. The Humphreys Family in America, 1883.

Hunt. Va. Co. Records, VI.

Hunter. Richmond, Va., Standard, III. Slaughter's Hist. of St. Mark's Par. Wm. and Mary Quar., II, VII, XVI. Va. Co. Records, I, II, VI. Lower Norfolk Co. Antiquary. Wheeler's Hist. of No. Carolina. Hist. of the Bulloch and Allied Families, by J. G. Bulloch, 1892. MSS. Ped. of the Genealogical Assn. Descendants of Samuel Hunter of Augusta Co., Va., by W. W. Ustick, 1895. Record of Hunter of Fairfax Co., Va., by Mary A. H. Bull, 1902.

Hunton. Philip Hunton and His Descendants, by D. T. V. Huntoon, 1881.

Hutcheson. Va. Co. Records, I, II.

Hutchins. Warfield's Hist. of Anne Arundel and Howard Cos., Md. Va. Co. Records, VI, VII. Va. Hist. Mag., XV. Lower Norfolk Co., Va., Antiquary.

Hutt. Wm. and Mary Quar., XV. Va. Co. Records, VI.

Hutton. Va. Co. Records, VI.

Hutson. So. Carolina Hist. and Genl. Mag., IX.

Hyde. Richmond Standard, II. Wm. and Mary Quar., I, VI, XIV. Va. Co. Records, I.

Hynson. Hanson's Hist. of Old Kent, Md.

Iglehart. Warfield's Hist. of Anne Arundel and Howard Cos., Md.

Ingles. Wm. and Mary Quar., VI, VII.

Inglis. Va. Co. Records, V.

Ingram. Middlesex, Va., Par. Reg. Va. Co. Records, VI.

Innes. Green's Kentucky Families. Meade's Old Fam. and Churches. Richmond Standard, III. The Willis Family of Va., by B. C. and R. H. Willis, 1898.

Inman. The Descendants of John Walker of Wigton and Va., by Emma S. White, 1902.

Irby. Meade's Old Fam. and Churches. Wm. and Mary Quar., V, VII. Va. Co. Records, IV.

Iredell. Wheeler's Hist. of No. Carolina.

Irvin and Irvine. Wood's Hist. of Albemarle. Sketches of Lynchburg, by Mrs. Julia M. Cabell. Green's Kentucky Families. The Irvines and Their Kin, by Mrs. L. Boyd, 1898, 2d enlarged Ed., 1908. Habersham Hist. Coll. of Ga. Hist. of the Bulloch and Allied Families, by J. G. Bulloch, 1892.

Irwin. Keith's Harrison Ancestry. Va. Co. Records, I. Wm. and Mary Quar., VIII. Wheeler's Hist. of No. Carolina. Va. Co. Records, I.

Isham. Richmond Standard, III. Va. Hist. Mag., IV, XVIII. Wm. and Mary Quar., I. Tyler's Cradle of the Republic. Va. Co Records, V.

Ives. Lower Norfolk Co., Va., Antiquary.

Izard. So. Carolina Hist. and Genl. Mag., II. Wm. and Mary Quar., VII.

Jack. Slaughter's Hist. of St. Mark's Par. Habersham Hist. Coll. of Ga., I.

Jackman. Va. Hist. Mag., XI.

Jackson. Wm. and Mary Quar.. XII, XIV. Va. Co. Records, I, II, VI, VII. Middlesex Par. Reg., Va. Goodwyn's Hist. of Bruton Church. St. Peter's Par. Reg., New Kent, Va. Chamberlayne's Bristol Par. Reg., Va.

Jacobs. Va. Co. Records, VI.

Jacquelin. Meade's Old Fam. and Churches. Va. Hist. Coll, V. Wm. and Mary Quar., IV, V. Tyler's Cradle of the Republic, 1906. Va. Co. Records, V. Some Prominent Va. Families, by Louise Pecquet du Bellet, 1907.

Jadwin. Va. Co. Records, V.

James. Richmond, Va., Standard, II. Va. Co. Records, I, II, VI. Middlesex Par. Reg., Va. Wm. and Mary Quar., V, VI. Lower Norfolk Co. Antiquary.

Jameson. Va. Co. Records, II, V, VI. Wood's Hist. of Albemarle, Va. Wm. and Mary Quar., II, III, VIII. The Jamesons in America, by E. O. Jameson, 1900.

Jamieson. Wm. and Mary Quar., XIII.

Janney. The Jolliffe Family of Va., by Wm. Jolliffe, 1893. The Thomas Family of Md., by L. B. Thomas.

Jarman. Wood's Hist. of Albemarle.

Jarratt. St. Peter's Par. Reg., New Kent, Va. Wm. and Mary Quar., XI.

Jeffries. Va. Co. Records, VI. Middlesex, Va., Par. Reg.

Jefferson. Campbell's Hist. of Va. Goode's Va. Cousins. Meade's Old Fam. and Churches. Randall's Life of Jefferson, I. Slaughter's Fry Gen. Wood's Hist. of Albemarle. Wm. and Mary Quar., VI. Middlesex Par. Reg., Va.

Jenifer. Hanson's Hist. of Old Kent, Md.

Jennings. Jennings Family Convention, Charlottesville, 1850. Wm. and Mary Quar., III, IV, VII, IX, X. Va. Hist. Mag., IV, VI, XII. Meade's Old Fam. and Churches. Richmond Standard, III. Va. Co. Records, I, V, VI, VII. Goodwyn's Hist. of Bruton Church. Lee of Va., by E. J. Lee, 1895.

Jenkins. Va. Co. Records, I, II. Wm. and Mary Quar., IX.

Jerdone. Wm. and Mary Quar., V, VI, VII, XI, XII. Va. Co. Records, V.

Jervey. So. Carolina Hist. and Genl. Mag., VII.

Jett. Va. Co. Records, V.

Johns. The Thomas Book, by L. B. Thomas, 1896.

Johnson. Warfield's Founders of Anne Arundel and Howard Cos., Md. The Thomas Book, by L. B. Thomas, 1896. The Buford Fam. in America, by M. B. Buford. Hanson's Hist. of Old Kent, Md. Munsell's American Ancestry, VII. Meade's Old Fam. and Churches. Richmond Standard, III. Slaughter's St. Mark's Par. Va. Hist. Mag., VII. Va. Co. Records, I, II, VI. Middlesex Par. Reg., Va. St. Peter's Par. Reg., New Kent, Va. Wm. and Mary Quar., V, VI, VII. Chamberlayne's Bristol Par. Reg.

Johnston. Richmond Standard, II. Slaughter's St. Mark's Par. Va. Hist. Mag., VII. Johnston's Old Va. Clerks. Va. Co. Records, I, II, VI. Middlesex, Va., Par. Reg. Chamberlayne's Bristol Par. Reg. Wheeler's Eminent No. Carolinians. Habersham Hist. Coll. of Ga., II.

Joliffe. The Joliffe Family of Va., by Wm. Joliffe, 1893.

Jones. Capt. Roger Jones of London and Va., by L. H. Jones, 1891. Meade's Old Fam. and Churches. Richmond Standard, II, III. Slaughter's Bristol Par. Slaughter's St. Mark's Par. Wm. and Mary Quar., I, II, IV, V, VII, VIII, IX, XI, XIII, XIV. Va. Hist. Mag., I, IV, V, VI, VIII. Green's Hist of Culpeper Co. Wood's Hist. of Albemarle Co. Va. Co. Records, I, II, IV, V, VI. Middlesex, Va., Par. Reg. Goodwyn's Hist. of Bruton Church. St. Peter's Par. Reg., New Kent, Va. Crozier's Buckners of Va., 1907. Chamberlayne's Bristol Par. Reg. Warfield's Founders of Anne Arundel and Howard Cos., Md. Lee of Va., by E. J. Lee. Green's Kentucky Families. Paxton's Marshall Family. The Thomas Family of Md., by L. B. Thomas. Wheeler's Eminent North Carolinians. Wheeler's Hist. of No. Carolina. Hist. of the Bulloch and Allied Families, by J. D. Bulloch. Jones Family of Va. and the Carolinas, by A. I. Robertson, 1900.

Jordan. Neill's Va. Carolorum. Va. Hist. Mag., IV. Middlesex, Va., Par. Reg. Wm. and Mary Quar., V, VII, XIII, XIV. Va. Co. Records, II, VI. Sketches of the First Families of Upper Georgia, by G. R. Gilmer, 1855.

Joslin. Oliver's Carter Family Tree.

Jouett. Wood's Hist. of Albemarle Co. Va.

Joyner. Meade's Old Fam. and Churches. Richmond Standard, II. Johnson's Old Va. Clerks.

Joynes. Wm. and Mary Quar., X.

Julian. Munsell's American Ancestry, VII. Va. Hist. Mag., V. Va. Co. Records, I.

Junkin. Genl. Chart of Junkin and Allied Families of Va., by F. T. A. Junkin, 2d Ed., revised, 1908.

Juxon. Wm. and Mary Quar., XVII. Va. Hist. Mag., XV.

Kane. The Thomas Family of Md., by L. B. Thomas.

Kay. Wm. and Mary Quar., VII.

Kearney. The Alstons of N. and S. Carolina, by J. A. Groves, 1902.

Keeble. Va. Co. Records, V.

Keeling. Richmond Standard, IV. Middlesex Par. Reg. Va. Hist. Mag., IV. Lower Norfolk Co., Va., Antiquary.

Keene. Wm. and Mary Quar., VIII, XVIII. Va. Hist. Mag., I.

Keith. Meade's Old Fam. and Churches, II. Goodwyn's Bruton Church. Va. Co. Records, VI. Green's Kentucky Families. Marshall Family of Va., by W. M. Paxton. Habersham Hist. Coll. of Ga., II. MSS. Ped. of the Genealogical Assn.

Keller. Richmond Standard, IV.

Kelly. Wm. and Mary Quar., XV, XVI. Wood's Hist. of Albemarle. Va. Co. Records, I, II, VI, VII.

Kelshaw. Middlesex, Va., Par. Reg.

Kempe. Va. Hist. Mag., II, III, VIII, X. Goodwyn's Bruton Church. Middlesex, Va., Par. Reg. Wm. and Mary Quar., II, III. Va. Co. Records, V, VI, VII.

Kemper. History of the Kemper Family (Va.), by W. M. Kemper and H. L. Wright, 1899.

Kendall. Wm. and Mary Quar., XVIII. Goodwyn's Hist. of Bruton Church. Va. Co. Records, VI.

Kennan. Paxton's Marshall Family of Va.

Kenner. Hayden's Va. Gen. Wm. and Mary Quar., VIII, IX, XVI, XVII, XVIII. Va. Hist. Mag., IX.

Kennon. Meade's Old Fam. and Churches. Richmond Standard, II. Robertson's Pocahontas' Descendants. Slaughter's Bristol Par. Va. Hist. Mag., V, XIII. Wm. and Mary Quar., III, V, XIV, XV. Chamberlayne's Bristol Par. Reg. Of Sceptred Race, by Annah R. Watson. Richmond Critic, 1888.

Kent. Warfield's Founders of Anne Arundel and Howard Cos., Md. The McGavock Family, by Rev. Robert Gray.

Kerby. Wm. and Mary Quar., XIV, XVII.

Kerr. Wood's Hist. of Albemarle. Richmond Standard, III.

Key. Hayden's Va. Gen. Richmond Standard, III. Wood's Hist. of Albemarle. Hanson's Hist. of Old Kent, Md. Paxton's Marshall Fam. Maryland Hist. Mag., V.

Kilgour. Some Va. Families, by H. M. McIlhany, 1903.

King. Meade's Old Fam. and Churches. Richmond Standard, II, III. Va. Hist. Mag., III. Wm. and Mary Quar., VII, XVI. Va. Co. Records, I, II, III, VI, VII. Middlesex, Va., Par. Reg. Hist. of S. W. Virginia, by L. P. Summers, 1903. Chamberlayne's Bristol Par. Reg. Thomas Family of Md., by L. B. Thomas.

Kingsmill. Wm. and Mary Quar., II, VI. Va. Co. Records, V.

Kinkead. Wood's Hist. of Albemarle.

Kinloch. Campbell's Spotswood Gen. Page Gen., by R. C. M. Page. Slaughter's Hist. of St. Mark's Par.

Kinney. Johnston's Old Va. Clerks. Some Va. Families, by H. M. McIlhany, 1903.

Kinsolving. Wood's Hist. of Albemarle.

Kirby. Warfield's Hist. of Anne Arundel and Howard Cos., Md.

Kirk. Va. Co. Records, VI. Green's Kentucky Families.

Kirtley. The Buford Family, by M. B. Buford, 1903.

Knight. Richmond Standard, III. Va. Co. Records, I, VI. Wm. and Mary Quar., VII. The Thomas Family of Md., by L. B. Thomas.

Knott. Va. Hist. Mag., IV.

Knowles. The Thomas Family of Md., by L. B. Thomas.

Knox. Hanson's Old Kent, Md. Slaughter's Hist. of Bristol Par. Richmond Standard, II.

Komer. Peyton's Hist. of Augusta Co., Va.

Lacy. Va. Hist. Collections, V. St. Peter's Par. Reg., New Kent, Va. Va. Co. Records, VI. MSS. Ped. of Genealogical Assn.

Ladson. Habersham Hist. Collections, Ga., I.

Ladd. The Family of John Ladd of Charles City, Va., by Warren Ladd, 1890.

Lamar. Va. Co. Records, V. MSS. Ped. of Genealogical Assn.

Lamb. Wm. and Mary Quar., III, VII.

Lamount. Lower Norfolk Co. Va. Antiquary.

Lancaster. Wm. and Mary Quar., XVII.

Land. Lower Norfolk Co., Va., Antiquary.

Landon. Meade's Old Fam. and Churches. Va. Hist. Mag., II. Va. Co., Records, V. Keith's Harrison Ancestry.

Lane. Richmond Standard, III. Va. Co. Records, I, II, VI, VII. Wm. and Mary Quar., XII, XIII, XVIII. Habersham Hist. Coll. of Ga., II. Lane of Wake Co., N. Carolina, by M. D. Haywood, 1900.

Langborne. Wm. and Mary Quar., IV, V, XI, XIX. Va. Co. Records, V.

Langford. St. Peter's Par. Reg., New Kent, Va.

Langhorne. Cabell's Sketches of Lynchburg. Crozier's Buckners of Va., 1907. Paxton's Marshall Fam. The Langhorne Family, MSS. Ped., by H. B. Mackay, in N. Y. Pub. Library, 1900.

Langley. Wm. and Mary Quar., XIII. Va. Co. Records, VI. Lower Norfolk Co., Va., Antiquary.

Langston. Richmond Standard, I.

Lanier. Meade's Old Fam. and Churches. Welle's Washington Gen. Wm. and Mary Quar., III, IV, XV, XVII. Habersham Hist. Coll. of Ga., I. Early Settlers of Alabama, by J. E. Saunders. Sketch of the Life of J. F. D. Lanier, 1871. Va. Co. Records, VI, VII.

Latane. Meade's Old Fam. and Churches. Va. Hist. Mag., VIII. Va. Co. Records, V.

Lawrence. Warfield's Hist. of Anne Arundel and Howard Cos., Md. The Thomas Book, by L. B. Thomas. Va. Co. Records, VI, VII.

Lawson. Va. Hist. Mag., IV, V. Lower Norfolk Co., Va., Antiquary. Middlesex, Va., Par. Reg. Wm. and Mary Quar., VI, XVIII. Va. Co. Records, II, V, VI, VII. Hanson's Old Kent, Md. MSS. Ped. of the Genealogical Assn.

Laydon. Va. Hist. Mag., V.

Ledbetter. Chamberlayne's Bristol Par. Reg.

Leake. Va. Hist. Mag., XI. Wood's Hist. of Albemarle. Wm. and Mary Quar., VI.

Lear. Wm. and Mary Quar., VII, IX. Va. Hist. Mag., XVII.

Leath. Chamberlayne's Bristol Par. Reg.

Lee. Campbell's Spotswood Gen. Campbell's Hist. of Va. Oliver's Carter Family Tree. Hayden's Va. Gen. Meade's Old Fam. and Churches. Richmond Critic, 30th July, 1888. Richmond Standard, I, III, IV. Slaughter's Bristol Par. Southern Bivouac, 1886. Wm. and Mary Quar., I, II, III, IX, X, XI. Va. Hist. Mag., V, VI. Va. Co. Records, I, II, V, VI, VII. Middlesex, Va., Par. Reg. Chamberlayne's Bristol Par. Reg. Of Sceptred Race, by Annah R. Watson. Lee Fam. of Va. and Md., by E. C. Mead, 1868. New Eng. Genl. and Hist. Reg., XXVI. Lee of Va., by Cassius F. Lee and J. Packard, 1872. Lee of Va., by J. Henry Lea, 1892. Lee of Eng. and Va., by the Rev. Frederick G. Lee, London, 1884. Some Notable Families of America, by Annah W. Watson, 1898. Lee of Va., by Edmund J. Lee, 1895.

Leftwich. Meade's Old Fam. and Churches. Va. Co. Records, V. Leftwich Gen. Chart, drawn by W. H. Abbott, 1903.

Legare. Richmond Standard, II. Legare Fam., by Mrs. E. C. K. Fludd, 1886.

Le Grand. Wm. and Mary Quar., IX.

Leigh. Richmond Standard, II, III, IV. Habersham Hist. Coll. of Ga., I.

Leiper. Campbell's Spotswood Gen. Richmond Standard, V. Founder of Anne Arundel Co., by J. D. Warfield. Thomas Fam. of Md., by L. B. Thomas.

Lemon. The Lemon Family of Va. and Illinois, by F. B. Lemon, 1898.

Lester. Bryant Lester of Lunenberg Co., Va., by T. McA. Owen, 1897.

Letcher. The Buford Family, by M. B. Buford, 1903.

Levert. Wm. and Mary Quar., V.

Levy. Wood's Hist. of Albemarle.

Lewelling. Wm. and Mary Quar., VIII. Va. Co. Records, VI, VII. Va. Hist. Mag., XIII.

Lewis. Campbell's Hist. of Va. Oliver's Carter Family Tree. Hayden's Va. Gen. Howe's Hist. Coll. of Va. The Lewis Fam. in America, by W. T. Lewis, 1893. Minor's Meriwether Gen. Peyton's Hist. of Augusta Co., Va. Richmond Standard, II, III, IV. Robertson's Pocahontas' Descendants. Crozier's Buckners of Va., 1907. A Royal Lineage, by Annah R. Watson, 1901. Chamberlayne's Bristol Par. Reg. Tyler's Cradle of the Republic, 1906. The Lewis and Kindred Families, by McAllister and Tandy, 1906. The Buford Family, by M. B. Buford. Of Sceptred Race, by Annah R. Watson, 1910. Some Notable Families of America, by Annah R. Watson, 1898. Sketches of the First Families of Upper Georgia, by G. R. Gilmer, 1855. Green's Kentucky Families. Paxton's Marshall Family. Jones Fam. of London and Va., by L. H. Jones, 1891. Bulloch Family of Ga., by J. G. Bulloch, 1892. Va. Co. Records, I, II, V, VI, VII. St. Peter's Par. Reg., New Kent, Va. Middlesex, Va., Par. Reg. Wm. and Mary Quar., I, II, III, IX, X, XI. Va. Hist. Mag., IV, V, VII. Slaughter's Fry Gen. Slaughter's Hist. of St. Mark's Par. Va. Hist. Register, V. Welle's Washington Gen. Wood's Hist. of Albemarle. The Lewis Congress at Belair, Spottsylvania Co., Va., 1894.

Lightfoot. Meade's Old Fam. and Churches. Slaughter's Fry Gen. Slaughter's St. Mark's Par. Wm. and Mary Quar., I, II, III, IV, VI. Green's Hist. of Culpeper Co., Va. Hist. Mag., V, VII. Va. Co. Records, I, II, V, VI. St. Peter's Par. Reg., New Kent, Va.

Ligon. Warfield's Anne Arundel and Howard Cos., Md. Saunder's Early Settlers of Alabama, 1899. Va. Co. Records, VI.

Lillard. Green's Hist. of Culpeper Co., Va.

Lilly. Wm. and Mary Quar., I.

Lindsay. The Lindsays of America, by Margaret I. Lindsay, 1889. Va. Hist. Mag., X, XI, XVIII. Wm. and Mary Quar., XVI. Wood's Hist. of Albemarle. Va. Co. Records, I, V, VI, VII.

Lingan. MSS. Ped. of the Genealogical Assn.

Lippitt. Richmond Standard, II, III.

Lipscomb. Old King William Homes and Families, by P. N. Clarke, 1897. Va. Co. Records, I, VI.

Lister. Wm. and Mary Quar., III. Va. Co. Records, V.

Little. Hist. of the Blair, Banister and Braxton Families, by F. Horner, 1898. Wm. and Mary Quar., XV.

Littlepage. Hayden's Va. Gen. St. Peter's Par. Reg., New Kent, Va. Old King William Homes and Families, by P. N. Clarke, 1897.

Littleton. Meade's Old Fam. and Churches. Wm. and Mary Quar., VIII, IX. Va. Hist. Mag., XVIII. New Eng. Hist and Genl. Reg., XLII. Va. Co. Records, V, VI.

Livingston. Wm. and Mary Quar., XIII. Va. Co. Records, I.

Lloyd. Va. Hist. Mag., III, V, XI. Wm. and Mary Quar., VIII. Va. Co. Records, V, VI, VII. Lower Norfolk Co., Antiquary. Hanson's Old Kent, Md. Warfield's Anne Arundel and Howard Cos., Md.

Lockey. Wm. and Mary Quar., III, VIII.
Lockwood. Slaughter's Hist. of St. Mark's Par., Va.

Logan. Richmond Standard, III. Green's Kentucky Families. The Descendants of John Walker of Wigton, by Emma S. White.

Lomax. Meade's Old Fam. and Churches. De Bowes' Review, XXVI. Wm. and Mary Quar., VIII, IX. Southern Bivouac, 1886. Middlesex, Va., Par. Reg.

Long. Slaughter's Hist. of St. Mark's Par. Va. Co. Records, I, II, VI. Middlesex Va., Par. Reg.

Lord. Va. Hist. Mag., I. Wm. and Mary Quar., XV. Va. Co. Records, VI.

Love. Wm. and Mary Quar., XIII. Habersham Hist. Coll. of Ga., I. Va. Co. Records, VI.

Lovell. Welle's Washington Gen. Va. Co. Records, I. Slaughter's Hist. of St. Mark's Par.

Lovett. Lower Norfolk Co. Antiquary.

Lowe. Warfield's Hist. of Anne Arundel and Howard Cos., Md. Saunder's Early Settlers of Alabama.

Lowndes. Warfield's Hist. of Anne Arundel and Howard Cos., Md. Lowndes of So. Carolina, by G. B. Chase, 1876. The Maryland Hist. Mag., II.

Lowry. Va. Co. Records, II, VI. Wm. and Mary Quar., XVI, XVIII. Va. Hist. Mag., IV.

Loyall. Middlesex, Va., Par. Reg. Va. Hist. Mag., XV.

Lucas. Va. Hist. Mag., III. Va. Co. Records, I, VI. St. Peter's Par. Reg., New Kent, Va.

Luck. Va. Co. Records, I.

Luckin. Va. Co. Records, V.

Ludlow. Wm. and Mary Quar., II. Va. Co. Records, V, VI. Thomas Fam. of Md., by L. B. Thomas.

Ludwell. Meade's Old Fam. and Churches. Richmond Standard, I. Southern Bivouac, 1886. Bruton Church, by Goodwyn. Va. Hist. Mag., I, IV, VII. Wm. and Mary Quar., I, III, VI, X. Va. Co. Records, V, VI. Lee of Va., by E. J. Lee, 1895. The Ludwell Genealogy, by Cassius F. Lee, in New Eng. Hist. and Genl. Reg., XXXIII.

Luke. Va. Hist. Mag., III. Wm. and Mary Quar., VII. Va. Co. Records, V, VI. Green's Kentucky Families.

Lundy. The Lundy Family, by W. C. Armstrong, 1902.

Lunsford. Southern Bivouac, 1886. Wm. and Mary Quar., III, VIII, IX. Va. Hist. Mag., XVII. De Bowes' Review, XXVI. Va. Co. Records, V.

Lyddall. Richmond Standard, I. Wm. and Mary Quar., VII, X. Va. Co. Records, V.

Lyde. Wm. and Mary Quar., VII.

Lyle. Richmond Standard, III. Munsell's American Ancestry, VII. Green's Kentucky Families.

Lynch. Cabell's Sketches of Lynchburg. Wood's Hist. of Albemarle. Wm. and Mary Quar., XIII.

Lyne. Richmond Standard, III.

Lynn. Va. Co. Records, I.

Lyons. Meade's Old Fam. and Churches. Richmond Standard, II, III.

Maben. Richmond Standard, IV.

McAllister. The Descendants of Col. Alex. McAllister of Cumberland Co., N. C., by Rev. D. S. McAllister, 1900.

Macauley. Wm. and Mary Quar., VII, XI, XII.

Macdonald. Munsell's American Ancestry, VII.

McClanahan. The McClanahans, by H. M. White, 1894.

Maccubin. Warfield's Hist. of Anne Arundel and Howard Cos., Md.

Macfarlane. The Woods-McAfee Memorial, by Woods and Durett, 1905.

Maclin. Wm. and Mary Quar., VII. Saunder's Early Settlers of Ala.

McCormick. The Scotch-Irish Families of McCormick, Stevenson, Bell and McKenzie, in N. C., Ky., Miss. and Texas, by Andrew P. McCormick, 1897.

Macmurdo. Slaughter's Hist. of St. Mark's Par.

Macon. Richmond Standard, III, IV. Slaughter's St. Mark's Par. Wm. and Mary Quar., VI, X, XI, XII, XIV. Va. Hist. Mag., X. Hist. of Albemarle Co., by Woods. St. Peter's Par. Reg., New Kent.

Madden. Campbell's Hist. of Va. Meade's Old Fam. and Churches. Slaughter's St. Mark's Par. Gilmer's Georgians. Paxton's Marshall Family.

Madison. Hayden's Va. Gen. Lewis Gen., by W. T. Lewis, 1893. Meade's Old Fam. and Churches. Wm. and Mary Quar., IV, VI, IX, XI, XII, XIV. Green's Hist. of Culpeper Co. Va. Hist. Mag., VI. Va. Co. Records, I, VI, VII. The Willis Fam. of Va., 1898. Some Notable Families of America, by Annah R. Watson. Green's Kentucky Families. MSS. Ped. of Genealogical Assn.

Magee. Va. Co. Records, I.

Magruder. MSS. Ped. of Genealogical Assn. Wood's Hist. of Albemarle.

Mahan. Richmond Standard, III.

Maitland. Chamberlayne's Bristol Par. Reg., Va.

Major. Va. Co. Records, VI.

Malbone. Lower Norfolk Co., Va., Antiquary.

Mallory. Va. Hist. Mag., III, VIII, XII, XIV, XV. Wm. and Mary Quar., I. Tyler's Cradle of the Republic. Va. Co. Records, V, VI. Descendants of Mordecai Cooke of Va., by W. C. Stubbs, 1896.

Maltby. Paxton's Marshall Family.

Mangum. Va. Hist. Mag., II.

Mann. Wm. and Mary Quar., III, VI. Chamberlayne's Bristol Par. Reg. Va. Co. Records, II, V. The Mann Family in America, by G. S. Mann, 1884.

Manning. Saunder's Early Settlers of Ala. Va. Co. Records, VI.

Mansell. Va. Co. Records, VI.

Manson. Wm. and Mary Quar., X.

Marable. Wm. and Mary Quar., VI, VII, XVII.

Marchant. Lower Norfolk Co., Va., Antiquary.

Mark. Wm. and Mary Quar., VI.

Markham. Va. Hist. Mag., V, VI. Wm. and Mary Quar., IV. Paxton's Marshall Family.

Marks. Richmond Standard, II. Wood's Hist. of Albemarle Co.

Marot. Wm. and Mary Quar., V, VI, VII. Letters and Times of the Tylers, by L. G. Tyler, 1897.

Marriott. Warfield's Founders of Anne Arundel and Howard Cos., Md.

Marsh. Va. Co. Records, I, VI. Warfield's Founders of Anne Arundel and Howard Cos., Md.

Marshall. Oliver's Carter Family Tree. Meade's Old Fam. and Churches. Richmond Standard, II, III, IV. Va. Hist. Mag., VI, XII. Va. Co. Records, I, VI. A Monograph of the Marshall Family, by T. McA. Anderson. Wm. and Mary Quar., IV, V, VII, X. Lee of Va., by E. J. Lee. Paxton's Marshall Family of Va.

Martain. Va. Hist. Coll., V.

Martian. Va. Hist. Mag., I, IV. Rootes Family, by W. C. Torrence, 1906. Wm. and Mary Quar., II, XIV.

Martin. Meade's Old Fam. and Churches. Minor's Meriwether Gen. Neill's Va. Carolorum. Richmond Standard, III. Wm. and Mary Quar., III, VII, IX, X, XI, XIII, XVIII. Va. Hist. Mag., VIII, XV. Wood's Hist. of Albemarle. Va. Co. Records, I, II, V, VI, VII, VIII. Middlesex, Va., Par. Reg. Goodwyn's Hist. of Bruton Church. St. Peter's Par. Reg., New Kent. Chamberlayne's Bristol Par. Reg. Hist. of S. W. Virginia, by L. P. Summers. The Gentry Family, by Richard Gentry, 1909. The Lower Norfolk Co., Va., Antiquary. Genl. Joseph Martin and the War of the Revolution in Am. Hist. Assn. Papers, 1894. The English Ancestry of Genl. Joseph Martin of Albemarle Co., Va., a MSS. Ped. in possession of the Genealogical Assn. The Martin Family, by S. D. Martin, Ky., 1857. The Martin Family of Goochland Co., Va., by Irene D. Gallaway. Warfield's Hist. of Anne Arundel and Howard Cos., Md. Of Sceptred Race, by Annah R. Watson. The Lewis Family, by W. T. Lewis, 1893.

Marye. Meade's Old Fam. and Churches. Richmond Standard, II. Va. Hist. Coll., V. Va. Co. Records, I.

Mason. Campbell's Hist. of Va. Oliver's Carter Family Tree. Hayden's Va. Gen. Meade's Old Fam. and Churches. Southern Bivouac, 1886. Va. Hist. Mag., II, IV. Va. Co. Records, I, II, V, VI, VII. Middlesex, Va., Par. Reg. Wm. and Mary Quar., IV. Lower Norfolk Co., Va., Antiquary. The Descendants of Mordecai Cooke of Va., by W. C. Stubbs. Lee of Va., by E. J. Lee. Hanson's Old Kent, Md. Paxton's Marshall Family. The Richmond Critic, 22d Oct., 1888. MSS. Ped. of the Genealogical Assn.

Massenburg. Wm. and Mary Quar., V.

Massie or Massey. Va. Co. Records, I, II, VI, VII. Middlesex, Va., Par. Reg. St. Peter's Par. Reg., New Kent. Goode's Va. Cousins. Meade's Old Fam. and Churches. Richmond Standard, III. Wm. and Mary Quar., V, XIII, XV.

Masten. Wm. and Mary Quar., V. Va. Co. Records, I.

Mathews or Matthews. Va. Hist. Mag., I, XV. Wm. and Mary Quar., III, V, VI. Va. Co. Records, I, II, VI, VII. Meade's Old Fam. and Churches. Peyton's Hist. of Augusta Co., Va. Middlesex Par. Reg. St. Peter's Par. Reg., New Kent, Va. Gilmer's Georgians. Munsell's American Ancestry, VII.

Matthias. Va. Co. Records, VI. Lower Norfolk Co., Va., Antiquary.

Maund. Wm. and Mary Quar., IX.

Maupin. Richmond Standard, I, II, III. Va. Hist. Mag., VIII. Wood's Hist. of Albemarle. The Gentry Family, by Richard Gentry. Goodwyn's Hist. of Bruton Church, Va.

Maury. Goode's Va. Cousins. Maury Gen. Slaughter's Fry Gen. Va. Hist. Coll., V. Wm. and Mary Quar., V, VI, X. Wood's Hist. of Albemarle. Va. Co. Records, I. Saunder's Early Settlers of Ala. Some Notable Families of America, by Annah R. Watson.

Mauzy. Va. Hist. Coll., V.

Maxwell. Lower Norfolk Co., Va., Antiquary.

May. Slaughter's Hist. of Bristol Par. Chamberlayne's Bristol Par. Reg. Va. Co. Records, I, II.

Mayer. The Maryland and Penna. Family of Mayer, by B. Mayer, 1878.

Mayes. Chamberlayne's Bristol Par. Reg.

Mayo. Warfield's Founders of Anne Arundel and Howard Cos., Md. MSS. Ped. of the Genealogical Assn. Meade's Old Fam. and Churches. Moore's Hist. of Henrico Parish, Va. Wood's Hist. of Albemarle. Middlesex Par. Reg., Va. Wm. and Mary Quar., VII. Va. Co. Records, V, VI.

McAdam. Wm. and Mary Quar., XI, XIII. The McAdam Family (Sheet), by Thos. L. Broun, 1906.

McAfee. The Woods-McAfee Memorial, by Woods and Durett, 1905.

McAllister. Lewis and Kindred Families, by J. McAllister and L. B. Tandy, 1906.

McAlpine. Green's Kentucky Families.

McCandlish. Wm. and Mary Quar., V.

McCarthy. Wm. and Mary Quar., VII.

McCarty. Meade's Old Fam. and Churches. Richmond Standard, III. Va. Hist. Mag., VII.

McCaw. Wm. and Mary Quar., VII.

McClanahan. Johnston's Old Va. Clerks. The Buford Family, by M. B. Buford. Paxton's Marshall Family.

McClarty. Hayden's Va. Gen. Green's Kentucky Fam.

McClung. Richmond Standard, II. Buford Family, by M. B. Buford. Paxton's Marshall Family. Green's Kentucky Families.

McClure. Richmond Standard, III. Green's Kentucky Families.

McClurg. Wm. and Mary Quar., I.

McCormick. Some Va. Families, by H. M. McIlhany, 1903. Genealogies and Reminiscences, by H. H. McCormick.

McCue. Peyton's Hist. of Augusta Co.

McDermott. Wm. and Mary Quar., VII.

McDonald. Richmond Standard, IV.

McDowell. Keith's Harrison Ancestry. Peyton's Hist. of Augusta Co. Richmond Standard, II, III. Va. Hist. Mag., VII. Green's Kentucky Families.

McGavock. The McGavock Family, by Rev. Robert Gray, 1903.

McGeehee. Richmond Standard, IV. Wood's Hist. of Albemarle. Saunder's Early Settlers of Alabama.

McGuire. Meade's Old Fam. and Churches. Richmond Standard, III.

McIlhany. Some Va. Families, by H. M. McIlhany, 1903.

McIntosh. Richmond Standard, III.

McKellem. Richmond Standard, III.

McKennie. Wood's Hist. of Albemarle.

McKenzie. Wm. and Mary Quar., VIII.

McKnight. Richmond Standard, III. Green's Kentucky Families.

McMillan. Wm. and Mary Quar., VII.

McNeill. Va. Co. Records, II.

McPheeters. Va. Hist. Mag., VI. Green's Kentucky Families.

McRae. Meade's Old Fam. and Churches. Richmond Standard, II, III.

Meade. Wm. and Mary Quar., VIII, XIII. Campbell's Hist. of Va. Goode's Va. Cousins. Meade's Old Fam. and Churches. Page Gen., by R. C. M. Page. Robertson's Pocahontas' Descendants. Va. Co. Records, VI.

Means. Munsell's American Ancestry, VII.

Meaux. Wm. and Mary Quar., XVI. St. Peter's Par. Reg., New Kent.

Meeres. Warfield's Anne Arundel and Howard Cos., Md.

Megginson. Robertson's Pocahontas' Descendants.

Melson. Va. Co. Records, III.

Menifie. Va. Hist. Mag., XIV. Va. Co. Records, V.

Mennis. Wm. and Mary Quar., VII.

Mercer. Warfield's Anne Arundel and Howard Cos., Md. Oliver's Carter Family Tree. Meade's Old Fam. and Churches. Richmond Standard, I, II. Va. Hist. Mag., XIV. Wm. and Mary Quar., XVII. Va. Co. Records, I, II, V, VI, VII. Life of Genl. Hugh Mercer, by J. T. Goolrick, 1906.

Meredith. Goode's Va. Cousins. Meade's Old Fam. and Churches. Richmond Standard, II. Slaughter's St. Mark's Par. Wm. and Mary Quar., V. Va. Co. Records, II, VI, VII.

Meriwether. Meade's Old Fam. and Churches. The Meriwethers and Their Connections, by L. H. A. Minor, 1892. The Minors and Meriwethers, by Minor Meriwether, 1895. Record of Nicholas Meriwether, by W. A. Griffith, 1899. Richmond Standard, III. Wm. and Mary Quar., VI, IX, XII, XIV, XVII. Va. Hist. Mag., V. Jones Gen., by L. H. Jones. Wood's Hist. of Albemarle Co. Va. Co. Records, I, V, VI, VII. Of Sceptred Race, by Annah R. Watson. Some Notable Families of America, by Annah R. Watson. Gilmer's Georgians.

Merrill. Slaughter's Hist. of St. Mark's Par.

Merriman. Va. Hist. Mag., V. Warfield's Anne Arundel and Howard Cos., Md. Va. Co. Records. VI.

Metcalf. Wm. and Mary Quar., V Va. Co. Records, V. Green's Kentucky Families.

Michaux. Meade's Old Fam. and Churches. Va. Hist. Mag., X. Va. Hist. Coll., V.

Michie. Wood's Hist. of Albemarle Co.

Micou. Meade's Old Fam. and Churches. Slaughter's Fry Gen. Green's Culpeper Co., Va. Va. Hist. Coll., V.

Middleton. Va. Co. Records, VI. So. Carolina Hist. and Genl. Mag., I.

Milburn. Munsell's American Ancestry, VII.

Milby. Wm. and Mary Quar., XVIII.

Miles. Va. Co. Records, VI, VII.

Milledge. Habersham Hist. Coll. of Ga., I. Munsell's American Ancestry, VII.

Miller. Richmond Standard, III. Va. Hist. Mag., X. Va. Co. Records, I, II, III, V, VI, VII. Middlesex Par. Reg. Wm. and Mary Quar., IX, XI. Lower Norfolk Co. Antiquary. Hist. of the Miller and Other Families, by W. H. Miller, 1907.

Mills. Wm. and Mary Quar., VI, VIII. Wood's Hist. of Albemarle, Va. Co. Records, I, VI, VII.

Milner. Wm. and Mary Quar., II, IX, XIV. Va. Hist. Mag., IV. Habersham Hist. Coll. of Ga., I. Va. Co. Records, V.

Milton. Some Va. Families, by H. M. McIlhany, 1903.

Minge. Oliver's Carter Family Tree. Meade's Old Fam. and Churches. Richmond Standard, II. Va. Hist. Mag., III. Wm. and Mary Quar., XV, XVI. Va. Co. Records, III.

Minitree. Richmond Standard, III.

Minor. Hayden's Va. Gen. Minor's Meriwether Gen. Meriwethers and Minors, by Minor Meriwether, 1895. Wm. and Mary Quar., VI, VIII, IX. Va. Hist. Mag., I, X, XI. Wood's Hist. of Albemarle. Va. Co. Records, I, II, V. Middlesex, Va., Par. Reg. Va. Hist. Coll., V. Paxton's Marshall Family.

Mitcham. Va. Co. Records, I. Middlesex, Va., Par. Reg.

Mitchell. Goode's Va. Cousins. Page Gen., by R. G. M. Page. Richmond Standard, II, III. Wm. and Mary Quar., X. Va. Co. Records, I, VI. St. Peter's Par. Reg., New Kent. Chamberlayne's Bristol Par. Reg.

Moffett. Peyton's Hist. of Augusta Co. Green's Kentucky Families.

Moncure. Hayden's Va. Gen. Meade's Old Fam. and Churches. Welle's Washington Gen. Crozier's Buckners of Va., 1907.

Monroe. Wm. and Mary Quar., IV, VII, XIV, XV, XVI. Wood's Hist. of Albemarle. Green's Kentucky Families.

Montague. Va. Co. Records, I, V. Middlesex, Va., Par. Reg. Wm. and Mary Quar., II. Gen. of the Montague Family, by Wm. L. Montague, 1886. Peter Montague of Va., and His Descendants, by G. W. Montague, 1894.

Montgomery. Green's Kentucky Families. Montgomery Fam. in Landrum's Hist. of Spartanburg Co., S. C.

Moon. Wood's Hist. of Albemarle. St. Peter's Par. Reg., New Kent. Wm. and Mary Quar., VII, XVII.

Moone. Va. Hist. Mag., V, VI. Va. Co. Records, VI.

Moore. Campbell's Spottswood Gen. Foote's Sketches of Va., 1st Series. Richmond Standard, II, III, IV. Slaughter's St. Mark's Par. Welle's Washington Gen. Wm. and Mary Quar., II, V, IX, XV, XVI, XVII. Wood's Hist. of Albemarle. Va. Co. Rec-

52   VIRGINIA COUNTY RECORDS.

ords, I, II, V, VI, VII. St. Peter's Par. Reg., New Kent, Va.
Chamberlayne's Bristol Par. Reg. Lower Norfolk Co., Va. An-
tiquary. John Walker of Wigton, Scotland and Va., by Emma S.
White, 1902. Green's Kentucky Families.

Moorman. Wood's Hist. of Albemarle Co.

Morris. Meade's Old Fam. and Churches. Wood's Hist. of Albe-
marle. Va. Co. Records, I, II, VI, VII. St. Peter's Par. Reg.,
New Kent. Wm. and Mary Quar., VIII. Paxton's Marshall
Family. The Thomas Family, by L. B. Thomas.

Mordecai. Wheeler's Hist. of N. Carolina.

Morecock. Wm. and Mary Quar., VII, XVI.

Morehead. Va. Co. Records, V, VI, VII.

Morrison. Southern Bivouac, 1886. Va. Co. Records, VI, VII. Morrison Family, by L. A. Morrison, 1880.

Morgan. Meade's Old Fam. and Churches. Va. Co. Records, II, VI,
VII. St. Peter's Par. Reg., New Kent. Paxton's Marshall Family. Maryland Hist. Mag., II.

Morse. Lower Norfolk Co., Va., Antiquary. Va. Hist. Mag., I.

Morson. Hayden's Va. Gen. Wm. and Mary Quar., II, X. Paxton's
Marshall Family.

Mortimer. Va. Co. Records, I.

Morton. Hayden's Va. Genl. Meade's Old Fam. and Churches. Rich-
mond Standard, II, III. Slaughter's St. Mark's Par. Va. Hist.
Mag., XI, XII, XVII. Wm. and Mary Quar., V, VI. Va. Co.
Records, I, VI, VII. The Pedens of America, by Eleanor M.
Hewell, 1900. The Ancestry of David Morton, by Daniel
Morton, 1901. The Mortons and Their Kin, by Daniel Morton,
1908. So. Carolina Hist. Mag., V.

Moryson. Wm. and Mary Quar., I, IV, IX. Va. Hist. Mag., II,
XIV. Va. Co. Records, V.

Mosby. Goode's Va. Cousins. Meade's Old Fam. and Churches. Richmond Standard, III. Slaughter's St. Mark's Par. Va. Hist. Mag.,
V, X. Va. Co. Records, VI, VII.

Moseley. Meade's Old Fam. and Churches. Wm. and Mary Quar.,
II, IV. Va. Hist. Mag., V. Va. Co. Records, I, II, VI, VII.
Middlesex, Va., Par. Reg. Lower Norfolk Co. Antiquary.
Wheeler's Hist. of No. Carolina.

Moss. Wm. and Mary Quar., VII. St. Peter's Par. Reg., New Kent.
Va. Co. Records, VI.

Mossom. Wm. and Mary Quar., II, V.

Mothershead. Va. Co. Records, IV.

Mott. Wm. and Mary Quar., XVI.

Mottrom. Wm. and Mary Quar., XVII.

Moultrie. So. Carolina Hist. Mag., VI.

Mountfort. Wm. and Mary Quar., VII.

Mouring. Wm. and Mary Quar., XII.

Moxley. Va. Co. Records, I.

Munden. Lower Norfolk Co. Antiquary.

Munford.   Bolling Gen.   Meade's Old Fam. and Churches.   Richmond Standard, I.   Slaughter's Hist. of Bristol Par.   Wm. and Mary Quar., VI, XI.   Chamberlayne's Bristol Par. Reg.

Murfree.   Wheeler's Hist. of No. Carolina.

Murphy.   Munsell's American Ancestry, VII.   Va. Co.   Records, II, VI, VII.

Murray.   Robertson's Pocahontas' Descendants.   Slaughter's Hist. of Bristol Par.   Lower Norfolk Co. Antiquary.   Va. Co. Records, II, VI.   Green's Kentucky Families.   Hanson's Old Kent, Md.

Murrell.   Goode's Va. Cousins.   Cabell's Sketches of Lynchburg.   Richmond Standard, III.

Muscoe.   Wm. and Mary Quar., XIII.

Musgrave.   Va. Hist. Mag., XIV.

Musick.   Lewis Gen. by W. T. Lewis, 1893.   Va. Co. Records, I.

Mutter.   Richmond Standard, III.

Nalle.   Va. Co. Records, II.   Hayden's Va. Gen.   Slaughter's St. Mark's Par.

Nance.   St. Peter's Par. Reg., New Kent, Va.   Chamberlayne's Bristol Par. Reg., Va.   The Nance Family of Pittsylvania Co., Va., by Geo. W. Nance, 1904.

Napier.   Habersham Hist. Coll. of Ga., I.

Nash.   Middlesex, Va., Par. Reg.   Va. Co. Records, II, VI, VII.   Wheeler's Hist. of No. Carolina.

Naylor.   Va. Co. Records, VI.

Neale.   Richmond Standard, III.   MSS. Ped. of Va. Hist. Society.   Wm. and Mary Quar., XVIII.   Neale Family of Md. (Sheet), by Dr. B. B. Browne, 1894.   Va. Co. Records, VI.

Needler.   Va. Hist. Mag., XIV.

Neil.   Paxton's Marshall Family.   Green's Kentucky Families.

Neilson.   Wood's Hist. of Albemarle.

Nelms.   Wm. and Mary Quar., XVIII.

Nelson.   Campbell's Hist. of Va.   Oliver's Carter Family Tree.   Goode's Va. Cousins.   Meade's Old Fam. and Churches.   Richmond, Va., Critic, 1888.   Richmond Standard, I, III.   Welle's Washington Gen.   Wm. and Mary Quar., II, IV, V, VI, VII, VIII, X.   Wood's Hist. of Albemarle.   Va. Hist. Mag., XIII, XVI, XVII.   Va. Co. Records, I, III, V, VI, VII.

Netherland.   Wm. and Mary Quar., V.   St. Peter's Par. Reg., New Kent.

Nevill.   Va. Hist. Mag., VI, VII, XVI.   Va. Co. Records, V, VI, VII.

Newce.   Wm. and Mary Quar., IX.   Va. Co. Records, V.

Newell.   Bulloch and Allied Families, by J. G. Bulloch, M.D., 1892.

Newman.   Slaughter's St. Mark's Par.   Gleanings of Va. History, by Wm. F. Boogher, 1903.   Wm. and Mary Quar., VII.   Va. Co. Records, VI.

Newsom.   Va. Hist. Mag., IV.   Slaughter's Hist. of St. Mark's Par.

Newton.   Meade's Old Fam. and Churches.   Wm. and Mary Quar., I, II, V, IX.   Va. Hist. Mag., I.   Va. Co. Records, I, V.   Middlesex, Va., Par. Reg.   Lower Norfolk Co. Antiquary.   Green's Kentucky Families.   Paxton's Marshall Family.

Nicholas. The Bclling Gen. Oliver's Carter Family Tree. Meade's Old Fam. and Churches. Richmond Standard, I, III. Slaughter's Fry Gen. Johnston's Old Va. Clerks. Wood's Hist. of Albemarle. Goodwyn's Hist. of Bruton Church. Wm. and Mary Quar., I. Richmond Critic, 30th Aug., 1890. MSS. Ped. of the Genealogical Assn.

Nicholls. Middlesex, Va., Par. Reg. Va. Co. Records, VI.

Nicholson. Wm. and Mary Quar., VI, XIII, XV. Goodwyn's Hist. of Brtuon Church. Va. Co. Records, V, VI, VII.

Nimmo. Wm. and Mary Quar., IV, V, VI, VIII, IX. Lower Norfolk Co., Va., Antiquary.

Nivison. Meade's Old Fam. and Churches.

Nix. Va. Co. Records, I.

Noel. Va. Co. Records, I.

Noland. Meade's Old Fam. and Churches.

Norman. Middlesex, Va., Par. Reg.

Norris. Va. Hist. Mag., I.

North. Johnston's Old Va. Clerks.

Norton. Richmond Standard, I, II. Slaughter's Fry Gen. Wm. and Mary Quar., X. Paxton's Marshall Family.

Norvell. Cabell's Sketches of Lynchburg, Va. Meade's Old Fam. and Churches.

Norwood. Warfield's Anne Arundel and Howard Cos., Md. Va. Hist. Mag., I, XIV.

Nosworthy. Wm. and Mary Quar., VII.

Nott. Va. Co. Records, V.

Nottingham. Va. Co. Records, VI, VII, VIII.

Nourse. Va. Hist. Mag., VIII. James Nourse and His Descendants, by Maris C. Nourse, 1897. Munsell's American Ancestry, VII.

Noye. Va. Hist. Mag., XIV.

Nunally. Chamberlayne's Bristol Par. Reg.

Nutt. Wm. and Mary Quar., XVIII.

Obenchain. Munsell's American Ancestry, VII.

Offley. Va. Hist. Mag., XII. MSS. Ped. of the Genealogical Assn. Va. Co. Records, V.

Ogle. Warfield's Anne Arundel and Howard Cos., Md.

Old. Wood's Hist. of Albemarle. Lower Norfolk Co. Antiquary.

Oldham. Wood's Hist. of Albemarle, Va.

Oliver. Richmond Standard, IV. Middlesex, Va., Par. Reg. Va. Hist. Mag., VI. Wm. and Mary Quar., VII. Chamberlayne's Bristol Par. Reg. Saunder's Early Settlers of Alabama. Va. Co. Records, VI, VII.

O'Neal. Va. Co. Records, I, II. Saunder's Early Settlers of Ala.

Opie. Wm. and Mary Quar., V, XI. Va. Co. Records, III. Va. Hist. Mag., XVIII.

Orgain. Wm. and Mary Quar., VIII.

Orrock. MSS. Ped. of the Genealogical Assn.

Osborne. Va. Hist. Mag., IV. Va. Co. Records, VI, VII. Wheeler's Hist. of No. Carolina.

Osburn. Munsell's American Ancestry, VII.

Otey. Wm. and Mary Quar., II. St. Peter's Par. Reg., New Kent. The Buford Family, by M. B. Buford, 1903.

Overby. Chamberlayne's Bristol Par. Reg.

Overton. Hayden's Va. Gen. Va. Hist. Mag., XI. Va. Co. Records, I, VI.

Owen. Cabell's Sketches of Lynchburg. Richmond Standard, III. Wm. and Mary Quar., II, IX. Va. Co. Records, I, II. Middlesex., Va., Par. Reg. Wheeler's Hist. of No. Carolina.

Owens. Lower Norfolk Co., Va., Antiquary.

Owings. Warfield's Anne Arundel and Howard Cos., Md.

Paca. MSS. Ped. of the Genealogical Assn. Warfield's Anne Arundel and Howard Cos., Md.

Pace. Middlesex, Va., Par. Reg.

Packe. Wm. and Mary Quar., III, VII.

Page. Gen. of the Page Family in Va., by R. C. Page, 1893. Oliver's Carter Family Tree. Meade's Old Fam. and Churches. Richmond, Va., Critic, 1888. Richmond Standard, III. Robertson's Pocahontas' Descendants. Wm. and Mary Quar., I, II, III, IV, VI, VII, XI. Wood's Hist. of Albemarle Co. Va. Co. Records, I, II, V, VI, VII, VIII. Goodwyn's Hist. of Bruton Church, Va. St. Peter's Par. Reg., New Kent. Lee of Va., by E. J. Lee. Welle's Gen. of the Page Family in England and America.

Paine. Va. Co. Records, I, VI, VII.

Palmer. Richmond Standard, III. Wm. and Mary Quar., II, VIII. IX. Va. Co. Records, VI, VII.

Panill. Richmond Standard, II, III. Wm. and Mary Quar., VI, XVI. Va. Co. Records, I.

Paradise. Wm. and Mary Quar., V, VI.

Parham. Chamberlayne's Brisol Par. Reg. Va. Co. Records, IV.

Parish. Va. Co. Records, I, II, IV, VI, VII. St. Peter's Par. Reg., New Kent.

Parke. Goodwyn's Hist. of Bruton Church. Va. Hist. Mag., XIII, XIV. Wm. and Mary Quar., II, III, X.

Parker. Meade's Old Fam. and Churches. Richmond Standard, I, III. Va. Hist. Mag., V, VI, VIII, XI, XVI. Va. Co. Records, I, III, IV, V, VI, VII. Wm. and Mary Quar., VII, XIII. Green's Kentucky Families.

Parks. Wm. and Mary Quar., VI, VII. Va. Hist. Mag., IX.

Parnell. Wm. and Mary Quar., VII.

Parrott. Middlesex, Va., Par. Reg.

Parry. Va. Co. Records, VI, VII.

Parsons. Chamberlayne's Bristol Par. Reg.

Partlow. Va. Co. Records, I.

Pasteur. Wm. and Mary Quar., III, V.

Pate. Wm. and Mary Quar., V, XII. The Buford Family, by M. B. Buford.

Paten. Richmond Standard, III.

Patteson. Wm. and Mary Quar., IV, VIII.

Patterson. St. Peter's Par. Reg., New Kent., Va. Wm. and Mary Quar., XIII. Chamberlayne's Bristol Par. Reg. John Walker of Wigton and Va., by Emma S. White, 1902. Va. Co. Records, II, VI, VII.

Patton. Richmond Standard, III. Slaughter's St. Mark's Par. Green's Kentucky Families.

Patrick. Wood's Hist. of Albemarle, Va.

Paul. Richmond Standard, II. Descendants of Mordecai Cooke of Gloucester Co., Va., by W. C. Stubbs. Va. Co. Records, II.

Pawlett. Wm. and Mary Quar., IV. Va. Co. Records, V.

Paxton. The Paxton Family, by W. M. Paxton, 1903. Wm. and Mary Quar., X. Green's Kentucky Families.

Payne. Hayden's Va. Gen. Slaughter's St. Mark's Par. Munsell's American Ancestry, VII. Va. Hist. Mag., V, VI, VII. Wm. and Mary Quar., II, VI, XVII. Va. Co. Records, I. Middlesex, Va., Par. Reg.

Peachy. Meade's Old Fam. and Churches. Wm. and Mary Quar., III, VI, XVII. Goodwyn's Hist. of Bruton Church. Va. Co. Records, II, III, V, VI, VII. Va. Hist. Mag., VII.

Peacock. Va. Co. Records, I.

Peale. Green's Kentucky Families.

Pearson. Hayden's Va. Gen. Richmond Standard, II, III. Wm. and Mary Quar., IV, X. St. Peter's Par. Reg., New Kent. Habersham Coll. of Ga., I. Va. Co. Records, V. Wheeler's Hist. of No. Carolina.

Peasley. St. Peter's Par. Reg., New Kent, Va.

Pebworth. Lower Norfolk Co., Va., Antiquary.

Peden. The Pedens of America, by Eleanor M. Hewell, 1900.

Pegram. Goode's Va. Cousins. Hayden's Va. Gen. Meade's Old Fam. and Churches. Richmond Standard, II. Slaughter's Bristol Par. Slaughter's St. Mark's Par., Va. Wm. and Mary Quar., XIV.

Peirce. Va. Co. Records, VI, VII.

Pelham. Wm. and Mary Quar., I.

Pemberton. Va. Co. Records, I. Old King William Homes and Families, by P. N. Clarke, 1897.

Pendarvis. The Genealogy of the Pendarvis-Bedon Families of So. Carolina, by J. B. Heyward, 1905.

Pendleton. Meade's Old Fam. and Churches. Slaughter's Hist. of St. Mark's Par., Va. Wm. and Mary Quar., X. Green's Hist. of Culpeper Co., Va. Va. Co. Records, I, II, V, VI. Goodwyn's Hist. of Bruton Church. MSS. Ped. of Genealogical Assn.

Penn. Meade's Old Fam. and Churches. Va. Co. Records, I. MSS Ped. of Genealogical Assn.

Pepper. Green's Kentucky Families.

Percy. Wm. and Mary Quar., II.

Perkins. St. Peter's Par. Reg., New Kent, Va. Va. Co. Records, VI, VII. Hanson's Old Kent, Md.

Perkinson. Chamberlayne's Bristol Par. Reg.

Perrin. Wm. and Mary Quar., III, V. Va. Co. Records, VI.

Perrott. Richmond Standard, IV. Wm. and Mary Quar., IV, VI. Va. Hist. Mag., V. Middlesex Par. Reg. Va. Co. Records, V. The Buford Family, by M. B. Buford.

Perry. Va. Hist. Mag., I. Wood's Hist. of Albemarle. Va. Co. Records, I, VI, VII. Wm. and Mary Quar., IV, VII, IX.

Pescud. Wm. and Mary Quar., XIV.

Peter. Va. Hist. Mag., IX. The Peter Family, Edition B, of the McDonald Gen., Ed. by Frank V. McDonald, 1880.

Peters. Va. Co. Records, VI.

Peterson. Richmond Standard, II. Slaughter's Bristol Par. Va. Co. Records, I, VI. Chamberlayne's Bristol Par. Reg.

Pettigrew. Wheeler's Hist. of No. Carolina.

Pettus. Moore's Hist. of Henrico Par., Va. Va. Hist. Mag., III. Wm. and Mary Quar., VI, X. Va. Co. Records, I, V, VI, VII.

Pettypool. Chamberlayne's Bristol Par. Reg.

Peyton. Hayden's Va. Gen. Meade's Old Fam. and Churches. Peyton's Hist. of Augusta Co., Va. Richmond Standard, II, III. Johnston's Old Va. Clerks. Wood's Hist. of Albemarle. Wm. and Mary Quar., III, VI. Va. Co. Records, V, VI, VII. MSS. Ped. of the Genealogical Assn.

Phelan. Saunder's Early Settlers of Alabama.

Phifer. Eminent No. Carolinians, by J. H. Wheeler, 1884.

Phillips. Meade's Old Fam. and Churches. Wm. and Mary Quar., XIII, XIV. Wood's Hist. of Albemarle. Va. Co. Records, I, II, VI, VII. Middlesex, Va., Par. Reg. Chamberlayne's Bristol Par. Reg.

Pickett. Wm. and Mary Quar., I. Va. Co. Records, II, VI. Green's Kentucky Families. The Allstons of No. and So. Carolina, by J. A. Groves, 1902.

Pierce. Meade's Old Fam. and Churches. Wm. and Mary Quar., IV, IX. Va. Hist. Mag., III. Goodwyn's Hist. of Bruton Church, Va. Va. Co. Records, II, VI, VII.

Pigg. Va. Co. Records, I, VI.

Piggot. Va. Co. Records, VI.

Pilson. Wood's Hist. of Albemarle Co., Va.

Pinchback. St. Peter's Par. Reg., New Kent, Va. Wm. and Mary Quar., XIII.

Pinckard. Wm. and Mary Quar., XII. Va. Co. Records, III. The Pinkard Family (Sheet), by Thos. L. Broun, 1906.

Pinkethman. Wm. and Mary Quar., VI. Goodwyn's Hist. of Bruton Church.

Pinkney. Warfield's Anne Arundel and Howard Cos., Md.

Piper. Wood's Hist. of Albemarle Co., Va.

Pitt. Wm. and Mary Quar., VII. Va. Co. Records, VI.

Pittman. Richmond Standard, III.

Pitts. Warfield's Anne Arundel and Howard Cos., Md. Va. Co. Records, I, VI.

Place. Va. Co. Records, V.

Plant. The House of Plant of Macon, Ga., by G. S. Dickerman, 1900.

Plantagenet. Richmond Standard, II.

Plater. Warfield's Anne Arundel and Howard Cos., Md. Maryland Hist. Mag., III, IV.

Pleasants. Meade's Old Fam. and Churches. Page Gen., by R. C. M. Page. Richmond Standard, II. Moore's Hist. of Henrico Par., Va. Va. Hist. Mag., IV, XVI, XVII, XVIII. Va. Co. Records, VI.

Plowden. Richmond Standard, II. MSS. Ped. of the Genealogical Assn.

Pocahontas. Pocahontas and Her Descendants through Her Marriage with John Rolfe, Gent., by Wyndham Robertson, 1887. The Bolling Gen. Goode's Va. Cousins. Richmond Standard, II, IV.

Poindexter. Wm. and Mary Quar., II. St. Peter's Par. Reg., New Kent. Va. Co. Records, VI. Sketches of the First Families of Upper Ga., by G. R. Gilmer, 1855.

Polk. The Descendants of John Walker of Scotland and Va., by Emma S. White, 1902. MSS. Ped. of the Genealogical Assn.

Pollard. Meade's Old Fam. and Churches. Richmond Standard, II. Wm. and Mary Quar., VIII, X, XV. Va. Co. Records, I, VI. St. Peter's Par. Reg., New Kent, Va.

Pollington. Neill's Va. Carolorum.

Poole. Va. Co. Records, I, VI.

Pope. Meade's Old Fam. and Churches. Richmond Standard, I, IV, VII, XII, XIII. Va. Hist. Mag., III. Va. Co. Records, VI. Munsell's American Ancestry, VII.

Porter. Richmond Standard, III. Va. Co. Records, I, VI. Middlesex, Va., Par. Reg. Lower Norfolk Co. Antiquary. Genealogies and Reminiscences, by Henrietta H. McCormick. Gen. of the Grigsby Family, including a Sketch of the Porter Family, by W. H. Grigsby, 1878.

Porterfield. Peyton's Hist. of Augusta Co., Va. Some Va. Families, by H. M. McIlhany, 1903.

Porteus. Wm. and Mary Quar., III, V.

Portlock. Lower Norfolk Co., Antiquary. Va. Co. Records, VI.

Posey. Goode's Va. Cousins. Meade's Old Fam. and Churches. Wm. and Mary Quar., V, VI. Va. Co. Records, I, II.

Pott. Richmond Standard, IV. Va. Hist. Mag., I. Wm. and Mary Quar., XIV. The Potts Family in Great Britain and America, by T. M. Potts, 1901.

Potter. Wm. and Mary Quar., XVIII. Va. Co. Records, VI.

Powell. Meade's Old Fam. and Churches. Slaughter's St. Mark's Par. Wm. and Mary Quar., V, VI, VII, VIII, XII. Va. Hist. Mag., I, V. Va. Co. Records, I, II, VI. Middlesex Par. Reg. Goodwyn's Hist. of Bruton Church, Va. Chamberlayne's Bristol Par. Reg. MSS. Ped. of the Genealogical Assn.

Power. Wm. and Mary Quar., I, VII. Va. Hist. Mag., XV.

Poythress. Goode's Va. Cousins. Meade's Old Fam. and Churches. Richmond Standard, I, II. Robertson's Pocahontas' Descendants. Slaughter's Hist. of Bristol Par. Va. Hist. Mag., VII, X. Chamberlayne's Bristol Par. Reg. MSS. Ped. of the Genealogical Assn.

Pratt. Warfield's Anne Arundel and Howard Cos., Md. Va. Co. Records, V.

Prentis. Meade's Old Fam. and Churches. Wm. and Mary Quar., II, VI, VII. Goodwyn's Hist. of Bruton Church. Va. Co. Records, V.

Presley. Wm. and Mary Quar., VIII.

Presson. Va. Co. Records, III.

Preston. The Preston Family of Va. and New Eng., by L. A. Wilson, 1900. Peyton's Hist. of Augusta Co., Va. Richmond Standard, I, II, III. Slaughter's Hist. of St. Mark's Par. Wm. and Mary Quar., II, III, VIII, XIII. Va. Hist. Mag., VII. Summer's Hist. of So. West Virginia, 1903. Warfield's Anne Arundel and Howard Cos., Md. Green's Kentucky Families. Hanson's Old Kent, Md. Paxton's Marshall Family. MSS. Ped. of the Genealogical Assn. Va. Co. Records, II.

Price. Meade's Old Fam. and Churches. Richmond Standard, III. Va. Hist. Mag., V, VI. Wood's Hist. of Albemarle. Va. Co. Records, I, II, VI, VII. Middlesex, Va., Par. Reg. Green's Kentucky Families. The Price Family of "Cool Water," Hanover Co., Va. (Chart), by T. H. and C. P. Price, 1906.

Prichard. Va. Co. Records, VI.

Pritchett. Va. Co. Records, I. Chamberlayne's Bristol Par. Reg.

Proctor. Va. Co. Records, I.

Prosser. Meade's Old Fam. and Churches. Va. Co. Records, VI.

Pryor. Va. Hist. Mag., V, VII. Middlesex, Va., Par. Reg. Wm. and Mary Quar., I, II, III, IV. Va. Co. Records, VI.

Puckett. Chamberlayne's Bristol Par. Reg.

Puddington. Warfield's Anne Arundel and Howard Cos., Md.

Pugh. Va. Co. Records, VI.

Pulliam. Va. Co. Records, I.

Purcell. Wm. and Mary Quar., IV.

Purdie. Richmond Standard, III. Wm. and Mary Quar., I, VII. Goodwyn's Hist. of Bruton Church. Va. Co. Records, III.

Purifoy. Descendants of John Purifoy, who were Confederate Soldiers, by F. M. Purifoy, 1904. Va. Hist. Mag., I, VII. Wm. and Mary Quar., VII, XVI.

Purnell. Richmond Standard, III.

Purvis. Va. Co. Records, I. Middlesex, Va., Par. Reg.

Puryear. Wm. and Mary Quar., V.

Putnam. History of Andrew Putnam of Washington Co., Md., by E. C. Wyand, 1909. Va. Hist. Mag., V. Wm. and Mary Quar., IV.

Quarles. Wood's Hist. of Albemarle. Va. Co. Records, I, VI. Old King William Homes and Families, by P. N. Clarke, 1897.

Quisenberry. Memoranda of the Quisenberry and Other Families, by A. C. Quisenberry, 1897. Memorials of the Quisenberry Family in Germany, England and America, by A. C. Quisenberry, 1900. Va. Co. Records, I, V.

Rae. Va. Co. Records, V.

Ragland. Habersham Hist. Coll. of Ga., I, II. Moore's Hist. of Henrico Par., Va. St. Peter's Par. Reg.

Ragsdale. Chamberlayne's Bristol Par. Reg.

Railey. Richmond Standard, II. Va. Hist. Mag., VII. Wood's Hist. of Albemarle.

Raines. Va. Co. Records, I, VI. Chamberlayne's Bristol Par. Reg.

Rainey. Lower Norfolk Co., Va., Antiquary.

Ramsay. Wood's Hist. of Albemarle. Va. Co. Records, V, VI.

Ramsey. Keith's Harrison Ancestry. Slaughter's Bristol Par.

Randall. Warfield's Anne Arundel and Howard Cos., Md.

Randolph. The Bolling Family, by Robert Bolling, 1868. Campbell's Hist. of Va. Oliver's Carter Family Tree. Goode's Va. Cousins. Hayden's Va. Gen. Cabell's Lynchburg Sketches. Meade's Old Fam. and Churches. Richmond, Va., Critic, 3d Sept., 1888. Richmond Standard, I, II, III. Robertson's Pocahontas' Descendants. Slaughter's Hist. of Bristol Par. Southern Bivouac, 1886. Johnston's Old Va. Clerks. Wm. and Mary Quar., I, II, IV, V, VII, VIII, IX, XI, XVII. Moore's Hist. of Henrico Par., Va. Va. Hist. Mag., III, VI, XIV. Wood's Hist. of Albemarle. Va. Co. Records, I, II, V, VI. Goodwyn's Hist. of Bruton Church. Tyler's Cradle of the Republic, 1906. The Thomas Book, by L. B. Thomas. Lee of Va., by E. J. Lee. Of Sceptred Race, by Annah R. Watson. Green's Kentucky Families. Paxton's Marshall Family. MSS. Ped. of the Genealogical Assn.

Ransome. Wm. and Mary Quar., X, XIV. Va. Hist. Mag., VIII.

Ravenel. History of the Huguenot Family of Ravenel of So. Carolina, by H. E. Ravenel, 1898.

Ravenscroft. Meade's Old Fam. and Churches. Va. Hist. Mag., IX. Wm. and Mary Quar., XVIII.

Rawlings or Rawlins. Warfield's Anne Arundel and Howard Cos., Md. Va. Co. Records, I, VI.

Rea. Wood's Hist. of Albemarle.

Read. Foote's Sketches of Va., 2d Series, I. Goode's Va. Cousins. Meade's Old Fam. and Churches. Richmond Standard, IV. Johnston's Old Va. Clerks. Va. Co. Records, VI.

Reade. Va. Hist. Mag., IV, VI. Wm. and Mary Quar., I, II, III, IV, IX, XI, XII, XIV, XV. Middlesex, Va., Par. Reg. Rootes Family, by W. C. Torrence. A Royal Lineage, by Annah R. Watson, 1901. Va. Co. Records, V, VI. Of Sceptred Race, by Annah R. Watson. Some Notable Families of America, by Annah R. Watson, 1898.

Redd. Va. Co. Records, I.

Reel. Munsell's American Ancestry, VII.

Rees or Reese. The Reese Family in Wales and America, by Mary E. Reese, 1903. Chamberlayne's Bristol Par. Reg.

Reeves. Va. Hist. Mag., XI. Va. Co. Records, I.

Reid. Wm. and Mary Quar., IV, VIII. Va. Co. Records, I, V. Lower Norfolk Co. Antiquary.

Renick. The Renick Family of Va., in Southern Hist. Assn. Pub.,
Vol. III, 1889. Va. Hist. Mag., X.

Ryner. Hanson's Old Kent, Md.

Reynolds. Wm. and Mary Quar., VIII, XII. Va. Co. Records, I,
IV, VI, VII. St. Peter's Par. Reg., New Kent, Va. Va. Hist.
Mag., VI.

Rhett. So. Carolina Hist. and Genl. Mag., IV.

Rhodes. Middlesex, Va., Par. Reg.

Rice. Richmond Standard, III. Green's Hist. of Culpeper Co., Va.
Va. Hist. Mag., VII, XIII. Va. Co. Records, I, II, V, VI, VII.
Middlesex, Va., Par. Reg.. Wm. and Mary Quar., XVIII.
Thomas Family of Md., by L. B. Thomas.

Rich. Va. Co. Records, V.

Richards. Va. Co. Records, I, V, VI, VII.

Richardson. Warfield's Anne Arundel and Howard Cos., Md. Thomas
Book, by L. B. Thomas. Munsell's American Ancestry, VII. Wm.
and Mary Quar., VI. St. Peter's Par. Reg., New Kent. Va. Co.
Records, II, VI, VII. The Richardson-De Priest Family, by R. D.
Roller, 1905.

Riddell. Richmond Standard, I.

Ridgeley. Warfield's Anne Arundel and Howard Cos., Md. MSS.
Ped. of Genealogical Assn.

Ridout. Warfield's Anne Arundel and Howard Cos., Md.

Riggs. Warfield's Anne Arundel and Howard Cos., Md.

Riley. Va. Co. Records, VI.

Rind. Wm. and Mary Quar., VII.

Ring. Wm. and Mary Quar., VI. Va. Hist. Mag., XIII. Va. Co.
Records, V.

Ringold. Hanson's Old Kent, Md. Bell Family of Hagerstown, Md.,
1894. Supplement of same, 1897.

Rives. Slaughter's Fry Gen. Wood's Hist. of Albemarle. Va. Co.
Records, VI. Chamberlayne's Bristol Par. Reg.

Roane. Meade's Old Fam. and Churches. Va. Hist. Mag., V, XVI.
Wm. and Mary Quar., IV, X, XVIII. Va. Co. Records, V. Middlesex, Va., Par. Reg.

Robards. Va. Hist. Mag., VII, VIII, IX, X, XI. Crozier's Buckners
of Va., 1907.

Robb. Va. Hist. Mag., X.

Roberson. Richmond Standard, III. Slaughter's St. Mark's Par.

Roberts. Va. Co. Records, I, II, VI, VII. Middlesex, Va., Par. Reg.
Goodwyn's Hist. of Bruton Church. St. Peter's Par. Reg., New
Kent. Chamberlayne's Bristol Par. Reg. Lower Norfolk Co.
Antiquary.

Robertson. Meade's Old Fam. and Churches. Richmond Standard,
II. Robertson's Pocahontas' Descendants. Slaughter's Bristol Par.
Slaughter's St. Mark's Par. Robertson's Gen. of King and Queen
Co., Va., by W. K. Anderson, 1900. Wm. and Mary Quar., III,
V. Va. Hist. Mag., V. Goodwyn's Hist. of Bruton Church.
Chamberlayne's Bristol Par. Reg. The Buford Family, by M. B.

Buford. Va. Co. Records, II, VI. The Family of Genl. James Robertson, by Lavinia R. Brown, in American Hist. Mag., I, II. 1896-7. Major Charles Robertson and Some of His Descendants, by Mrs. Charles F. Henley, in American Hist. Mag., III, 1898.

Robins. Neill's Va. Carolorum. Richmond Standard, II, III. Va. Hist. Mag., II. Va. Co. Records, I, III, VI. Wm. and Mary Quar., III.

Robinson. Campbell's Hist. of Va. Oliver's Carter Tree. Meade's Old Fam., and Churches. Richmond Standard, I, II, III, IV. Johnston's Old Va. Clerks. Va. Hist. Mag., III, VII, X, XV, XVI, XVII, XVIII. Wm. and Mary Quar., II, III, IV, VIII, X, XI, XVII, XVIII. Va. Co. Records, I, II, III, V, VI, VII. Middlesex, Va., Par. Reg. Chamberlayne's Bristol Par. Reg. Goodwyn's Hist. of Bruton Church. The Alstons of No. and So. Carolina, by J. A. Groves, 1902.

Rochefort. Va. Co. Records, VI.

Rodes. Va. Hist. Mag., VI, VII, IX. Wood's Hist. of Albemarle. Va. Co. Records, V. Middlesex, Va., Par. Reg.

Rogers. Underwood and Rogers Families, by J. C. Underwood, MSS. Coll. of the Va. Hist. Society. Some Va. Families, by H. M. McIlhany, 1903. Wood's Hist. of Albemarle. Va. Co. Records, I, II, VI. Wm. and Mary Quar., VI, VIII, XII.

Rolfe. Bolling Gen. Neill's Va. Carolorum. Richmond Standard, IV. Robertson's Pocahontas' Descendants. Va. Hist. Mag., I, IV. Wm. and Mary Quar., X. Va. Co. Records, V. Paxton's Marshall Family.

Rookins. Va. Hist. Mag., V, XI. Wm. and Mary Quar., VII, XII.

Rootes. Va. Hist. Mag., IV. Va. Co. Records, I, V. Rootes Family of Va., by W. C. Torrence, 1906. Wm. and Mary Quar., VII, XII.

Roper. St. Peter's Par. Reg., New Kent.

Roscaw. Va. Hist. Mag., VII. Va. Co. Records, V.

Rose. Meade's Old Fam. and Churches. Richmond Standard, I, II, III, IV. Slaughter's St. Mark's Par. Va. Co. Records, I, VI. Chart of the Ancestors of the Rev. Robert Rose of Va., by W. G. Stanard, 1895. Of Sceptred Race, by Annah R. Watson, 1910.

Rosewell. Hanson's Old Kent, Md.

Rosier. Wm. and Mary Quar., IV. Va. Co. Records, VI.

Ross. Va. Co. Records, I, II. Middlesex Par. Reg. St. Peter's Par. Reg., New Kent. Wm. and Mary Quar., X. Hanson's Old Kent, Md.

Rothery. Va. Co. Records, VI.

Rowe. Middlesex, Va., Par. Reg.

Rowland. Richmond Standard, II. Chamberlayne's Bristol Par. Reg.

Rowzie. Va. Co. Records, I, VI. Wm. and Mary Quar., VIII.

Roy. Meade's Old Fam. and Churches. Richmond Standard, II. Va. Hist. Mag., VIII. Va. Co. Records, I.

Royal. Cabell's Sketches of Lynchburg, Va. Meade's Old Fam. and Churches. Va. Hist. Mag., VIII, IX. Chamberlayne's Bristol Par. Reg. Va. Co. Records, VI. Paxton's Marshall Family.

Royle. Wm. and Mary Quar., VII, XIV.

Rucker. Va. Co. Records, I, VI.

Ruckes. Richmond Standard, III.

Ruffin. Meade's Old Fam. and Churches. Page Gen. Richmond Standard, II. Slaughter's Bristol Par. Va. Hist. Mag., V. Va. Co. Records, III. Wm. and Mary Quar., VII, XVIII. Richmond Critic, 19th Oct., 1889.

Ruggles. Wm. and Mary Quar., V.

Runkle. The Runkle Family in Europe and Their Descendants in America, by B. Van Doren Fisher, 1899.

Russell. Meade's Old Fam. and Churches. Richmond Standard, III. Wm. and Mary Quar., XI. Va. Co. Records, I, II, VI. Summer's Hist. of So. West Virginia, 1903. Goodwyn's Hist. of Bruton Church. Thomas Family of Md., by L. B. Thomas.

Rutherford. Richmond Standard, II. Va. Hist. Mag., VI, VII. Wm. and Mary Quar., I. The Thomas Family of Md., by L. B. Thomas.

Rutland. Warfield's Anne Arundel and Howard Cos., Md. The Thomas Book, by L. B. Thomas, 1896.

Ryedale. The Ryedales and Their Descendants in Great Britain and America, by G. T. Ridlon, 1884.

Ryland. Munsell's American Ancestry, VII

Sadler. Middlesex, Va., Par. Reg.

Safford. Richmond Standard, III.

Sailor. The Bell Family of Hagerstown, Md., 1894.

Sale. Va. Co. Records, I.

Salesbury. Va. Co. Records, VI.

Salle. Va. Hist. Collections, V.

Samms. Va. Co. Records, I.

Sampson. Richmond Standard, II. Wood's Hist. of Albemarle. Wm. and Mary Quar., VII.

Sanders. Va. Co. Records, I, II, VI. Middlesex Par. Reg. St. Peter's Par. Reg., New Kent.

Sanford or Sandford. Wm. and Mary Quar., II, IV. Va. Hist. Mag., XI. Va. Co. Records, VI. Middlesex Par. Reg.

Sandys. Neill's Va. Carolorum. Wm. and Mary Quar., II. Va. Co. Records, V.

Sappington. Warfield's Anne Arundel and Howard Cos., Md.

Saunders. Meade's Old Fam. and Churches. Richmond Standard, II. Va. Hist. Mag., XI. Wm. and Mary Quar., IV, VII, XIV. Va. Co. Records, I, VI. Goodwyn's Hist. of Bruton Church. Crozier's Hist. of the Buckners of Va. Saunder's Early Settlers of Alabama. Wheeler's Eminent North Carolinians, 1884.

Savage. Meade's Old Fam. and Churches. Va. Hist. Mag., I. Wm. and Mary Quar., XVI. Va. Co. Records, II, VI.

Sayer. Va. Hist. Mag., VI. Va. Co. Records, II.

Sayre. Va. Hist. Mag., III.

Scarborough. Hayden's Va. Gen. Meade's Old Fam. and Churches. Wm. and Mary Quar., VII. Va. Hist. Mag., IV, XVII. Middlesex Par. Reg. Va. Co. Records, II, V, VI.

Sayler. The Sayler Family of Maryland, by J. L. Sayler, 1898.

Schenck. Wood's Hist. of Albemarle.

Sclater. Wm. and Mary Quar., II, IV.

Scoggin. Chamberlayne's Bristol Par. Reg.

Scott. Hayden's Va. Gen. Meade's Old Fam. and Churches. Slaughter's St. Mark's Par. Wm. and Mary Quar., II, V, XIV. Wood's Hist. of Albemarle. Va. Co. Records, I, II, V, VI. St. Peter's Par. Reg., New Kent.

Screven. Hayden's Va. Gen. Two Centuries of the Baptist Church in So. Carolina, by H. A. Tupper, 1889.

Scrosby. Middlesex, Va.; Par. Reg. Va. Co. Records, III.

Scruggs. St. Peter's Par. Reg., New Kent.

Sears. Middlesex Par. Reg.

Seaton. Richmond Standard, III. Va. Co. Records, I.

Seaward. Middlesex Par. Reg. Wm. and Mary Quar., VII. Va. Co. Records, VI.

Seawell. Wm. and Mary Quar., III, IV, VII, VIII, XVII.

Seddon. Richmond Standard, II.

Segar. Va. Hist. Mag., V. Wm. and Mary Quar., II.

Selden. Hayden's Va. Gen. Meade's Old Fam. and Churches. Richmond Standard, II, III. Wm. and Mary Quar., V, VI, VII, IX, XII, XIV. Lower Norfolk Co. Antiquary.

Sellman. Warfield's Anne Arundel and Howard Cos., Md.

Semple. Robertson Family, by W. K. Anderson, 1900. Va. Co. Records, I.

Seneca. Lower Norfolk Co. Antiquary.

Servant. Wm. and Mary Quar., IX.

Seton. History of the Bulloch and Allied Families, by J. G. Bulloch.

Sewall. Maryland Hist. and Genl. Mag., IV.

Seward. Va. Hist. Mag., X.

Sewell. Warfield's Anne Arundel and Howard Cos., Md.

Sexton. Richmond Standard, II.

Shackelford. Richmond Standard, III. Slaughter's St. Mark's Par. Va. Co. Records, I. Middlesex Par. Reg.

Sharp or Sharpe. Va. Co. Records, I, II, VI. Richmond Standard, III. St. Peter's Par. Reg., New Kent. Sharpe Gen., by W. C. Sharpe, 1880.

Sheild. Wm. and Mary Quar., I, III, IV, V. Va. Co. Records, V.

Sheilds. Wm. and Mary Quar., V, VI, VII.

Sheldon. Va. Hist. Mag., XV. Wm. and Mary Quar., II.

Shelton. Richmond Standard, III. Wood's Hist. of Albemarle. Middlesex Par. Reg. Wm. and Mary Quar., VI. Va. Co. Records, VI. Early Settlers of Alabama, by J. E. Saunders, 1899.

Shepherd. Meade's Old Fam. and Churches. Va. Hist. Mag., III. Va. Co. Records, I, II, VI. Middlesex Par. Reg. Lower Norfolk Co. Antiquary. Gen. of the Duke, Shepherd and Van Metre Families, by S. G. Smyth, 1909. Lee of Va., by E. J. Lee.

Sheppard. Va. Co. Records, I, VI. Wm. and Mary Quar., VI, XIII.

Sherman. St. Peter's Par. Reg., New Kent. Va. Co. Records, III.

Sherwood. Lower Norfolk Co. Antiquary.

Shields. Richmond Standard III. Goodwyn's Hist. of Bruton Church. Wm. and Mary Quar., XVII. Letters and Times of the Tylers, by L. G. Tyler, 1897.

Ship. Va. Co. Records, I.

Shipley. Warfield's Anne Arundel and Howard Cos., Md.

Shipp. Lower Norfolk Co. Antiquary.

Shippen. Lee of Va., by E. J. Lee, 1895. Oliver's Carter Family Tree. Balch's Provincial Papers. Hanson's Old Kent, Md.

Shippey. Va. Hist. Mag., VI.

Shirley. Va. Co. Records, I.

Shivers. Habersham Hist. Coll. of Ga., I.

Short. Meade's Old Fam. and Churches. Wm. and Mary Quar., IV.

Sibley. Middlesex, Va., Par. Reg.

Sibsey. Va. Hist. Mag., VIII.

Sidway. Va. Hist. Mag., XIII.

Simmons. Va. Co. Records, I, II, VI. Lower Norfolk Co., Antiquary.

Simonson. Richmond Standard, III.

Simms. Richmond Standard, III. Wood's Hist. of Albemarle. Va. Co. Records, I, VI.

Simpson. Va. Co. Records, I, II, VI.

Skelton. Campbell's Hist. of Va. Meade's Old Fam. and Churches. Richmond Standard, III. Wm. and Mary Quar., II, VI, XII. Va. Co. Records, V. Jones Gen. of Va., by L. H. Jones, 1891.

Skinner. Va. Co. Records, VI.

Skipwith. Meade's Old Fam. and Churches. Robertson's Pocahontas' Descendants. Slaughter's Bristol Par. Southern Bivouac, 1886. Middlesex Par. Reg. Wm. and Mary Quar., II, VI, VII. Va. Co. Records, V.

Skyrme. Richmond Standard, IV. Slaughter's Fry Gen.

Skyren. Meade's Old Fam. and Churches.

Slaughter. Meade's Old Fam. and Churches. Richmond Standard, III. Slaughter's St. Mark's Par. Va. Hist. Mag., III, V, XVII, Green's Hist. of Culpeper Co. St. Peter's Par. Reg., New Kent. Va. Co. Records, I, II, V. VI.

Slingsby. The Coghill and Slingsby Families, by J. H. Coghill, 1879.

Smallwood. Va. Co. Records, I. Warfield's Anne Arundel and Howard Cos., Md.

Smart. Wm. and Mary Quar., III, VII.

Smelt. Meade's Old Fam. and Churches.

Smith. Goode's Va. Cousins. Hayden's Va. Gen. Neill's Va. Carolorum. Richmond Standard, III, IV. Slaughter's St. Mark's Par. Wm. and Mary Quar., II, IV, V, VI, VII, IX, X, XI, XII, XIII. Va. Hist. Mag., I, II, III, V, VI, VII. Gleanings of Va. History, by Wm. M. Boogher, 1903. Wood's Hist. of Albemarle. Va. Co. Records, I, II, III, IV, V, VI, VII. St. Peter's Par. Reg., New Kent. Middlesex Va. Par. Reg. Goodwyn's Hist. of Bruton Church. Chamberlayne's Bristol Par. Reg. Lower Norfolk Co. Antiquary. Of Sceptred Race, by Annah R. Watson, 1910. Maryland Hist. Mag., IV. So. Carolina Hist. and Genl. Reg., IV.

Smithers. Va. Co. Records, I. St. Peter's Par. Reg., New Kent Co.

Snead. Wm. and Mary Quar., X. Va. Co. Records, VI.

Snowden. Warfield's Anne Arundel and Howard Cos., Md. The Thomas Book, by L. B. Thomas.

Soblett. Va. Hist. Collections, V.

Somerville. Hayden's Va. Gen. Green's Hist. of Culpeper Co., Va. Co. Records, I.

Southall. Goode's Va. Cousins. Richmond Standard, II, III. Wm. and Mary Quar., VII, XII, XIII. Munsell's American Ancestry, VII. Wood's Hist. of Albemarle. Goodwyn's Hist. of Bruton Church.

Southey. Wm. and Mary Quar., VI.

Soutter. Richmond Standard, II.

Sowell. Wood's Hist. of Albemarle.

Spain. Chamberlayne's Bristol Par. Reg.

Spalding. Edward Spalding of Va. and Mass. Bay and his descendants, by C. W. Spalding, 1897.

Spamgler. Wm. and Mary Quar., VII.

Spann. Hayden's Va. Gen.

Sparks. Va. Co. Records, I.

Sparrow. Va. Co. Records, VI.

Speed. Richmond Standard, III. Slaughter's Fry Gen. Records of the Speed Family, by Thos. W. Speed, 1892. Saunder's Early Settlers of Ala.

Speke. Hayden's Va. Gen. Wm. and Mary Quar., IV.

Spelman. Wm. and Mary Quar., IV, XIV, XVII. Va. Hist. Mag., XV. Va. Co. Records, V.

Spence. Hanson's Old Kent, Md.

Spencer. Meade's Old Fam. and Churches. Va. Hist. Mag., II, IV, XVII. Wm. and Mary Quar., IV, VI, VII, X, XVII. St. Peter's Par. Reg., New Kent. Va. Co. Records, V, VI.

Spicer. Va. Hist. Mag., II. Wm. and Mary Quar., III, VI, XVII. Va. Co. Records, VI.

Spilman. Va. Hist. Mag., I. Wm. and Mary Quar., XIV.

Spiltimber. Wm. and Mary Quar., VII.

Spindle. Va. Co. Records, I.

Spooner. Va. Co. Records, I.

Spotswood. Campbell's Hist. of Va. Spotswood Gen., by Charles Campbell, 1868. Goode's Va. Cousins. Meade's Old Fam. and Churches. The Lindsays of America, by Margaret I. Lindsay, 1889. Richmond Standard, II, III, IV. Slaughter's Hist. of St. George's Par. Va. Slaughter's Hist. of St. Mark's Par. Va. Welle's Washington Gen. Green's Hist of Culpeper Co. Va. Co. Records, I, V. Wm. and Mary Quar., II, X. Goodwyn's Hist. of Bruton Church.

Spratt. Va. Co. Records, III.

Sprigg. Warfield's Anne Arundel and Howard Cos., Md. MSS. Ped. of the Genealogical Assn.

Stafford. Va. Hist. Mag. II.

Stanard. Meade's Old Fam. and Churches. Va. Hist. Mag., III. Va. Co. Records, I. Middlesex Par. Reg. The Thomas Book.

Stanley. Slaughter's Hist. of Bristol Par.

Stanton. Va. Co. Records, VI.

Staples. Johnston's Old Va. Clerks. Wood's Hist. of Albemarle.

Stark. Wm. and Mary Quar., XI.

Starke. Richmond Standard, III. Wm. and Mary Quar., IV, V, VII, XI. Va. Co. Records, I, III. Chamberlayne's Bristol Par. Reg.

Starkey. Richmond Standard, II, III.

Stavely. Hanson's Old Kent, Md.

Stears. Va. Co. Records, I.

Stedman. Wm. and Mary Quar., VIII.

Steel. Va. Co. Records, II, VI. Hanson's Old Kent, Md.

Stegg. Va. Hist. Mag., VI. Va. Co. Records, VI.

Steiner. Munsell's American Ancestry, VII.

Stephen. Va. Hist. Mag., XI, XVI. Va. Co. Records, II.

Stephens. Va. Hist. Mag., I. Va. Co. Records, I, II, VI. The Stephens Family of Va., Ky. and No. Carolina, by E. S. Clark, 1892.

Stephenson. Va. Co. Records, II, VI. Genealogical Records of Wm. Stephenson and His Descendants, by Mrs. E. M. S. Fite, 1905.

Steptoe. Meade's Old Fam. and Churches. Richmond Standard, III. Johnston's Old Va. Clerks. Va. Hist. Mag., VIII. Va. Co. Records, V.

Stevens. Warfield's Anne Arundel and Howard Cos., Md. Neill's Va. Carolorum. Slaughter's St. Mark's Par. Va. Co. Records, I, VI. Middlesex, Va., Par. Reg.

Stevenson. Meade's Old Fam. and Churches. Slaughter's St. Mark's Par. Green's Hist. of Culpeper Co. Some Va. Families, by H. M. McIlhany, 1903. Wood's Hist. of Albemarle. Va. Co. Records, I, II.

Steward. Chamberlayne's Bristol Par. Reg. Va. Co. Records, I.

Stewart. Middlesex, Va., Par. Reg. Chamberlayne's Bristol Par. Reg. Va. Co. Records, II, VI, VII. Hanson's Old Kent, Md. The Bulloch and Allied Families, by Joseph G. Bulloch, 1892.

Stiles. Wm. and Mary Quar., VIII. The Stiles Family in America, by Henry R. Stiles, 1895. A History of the Kentucky and Missouri Stiles Family, by La Fayette S. Pence, 1896.

Stith. Goode's Va. Cousins. Meade's Old Fam. and Churches. Richmond Standard, I. Johnston's Old Va. Clerks. Va. Hist. Mag., III, VII, VIII. Wm. and Mary Quar., I, III, IV, V, VI, VII, X, XVI. Moore's Hist. of Henrico Par., Va. Crozier's Buckner Family of Va., 1907. Chamberlayne's Bristol Par. Reg. Va. Co. Records, V. Richmond Critic, 27th Sept., 1890.

Stobo. Bulloch and Allied Families, by J. G. Bulloch, 1892. Va. Co. Records, II.

Stockett. Warfield's Anne Arundel and Howard Cos., Md.

Stockton. Wood's Hist. of Albemarle. Va. Hist Mag., II. Wm. and Mary Quar., IX.

Stokes. Meade's Old Fam. and Churches. **Va.** Hist. Mag., I, III, VI. Va. Co. Records, VI, VII.

Stone. Hayden's Va. Gen. Va. Hist. Mag., III, X, XII. St. Peter's Par. Reg., New Kent. Va. Co. Records, II, V, VI, VII. Lower Norfolk Co. Antiquary. Hanson's Old Kent, Md.

Storke. Wm. and Mary Quar., IV.

Storrow. Slaughter's St. Mark's Par., Va.

Stott. Va. Co. Records, VI.

Stover. Wm. and Mary Quar., IV.

Strachan. Richmond Standard, III. Va. Co. Records, I, V.

Strachey. Wm. and Mary Quar., II, III, IV, V, X. Va. Hist. Mag., XVIII. Va. Co. Records, V.

Strange. Robertson's Pocahontas' Descendants. Va. Co. Records, VI. St. Peter's Par. Reg., New Kent.

Stratton. Va. Co. Records, VI.

Straughan. Middlesex, Va., Par. Reg. Va. Co. Records, I.

Street. The Street Genealogy, by Mrs. Mary A. and Henry A. Street, 1895.

Stribling. Some Va. Families, by H. M. McIlhany, 1903.

Stringer. Va. Co. Records, VI.

Stringfellow. Slaughter's Hist. of St. Mark's Par., Va.

Strother. Meade's Old Fam. and Churches. Slaughter's St. Mark's Par. Green's Hist. of Culpeper Co., Va. William Strother of Va., and His Descendants, by Thos. McAdory Owen, in Southern Hist. Assn. Publications, April, 1898. Va. Co. Records, I, V, VI, VII. Crozier's Hist. of the Buckners of Va., 1907. Wm. and Mary Quar., XII. Some Notable Families of America, by Annah R. Watson. The First Families of Upper Georgia, by G. R. Gilmer, 1855. Green's Kentucky Families. Paxton's Marshall Family.

Stroud. Chamberlayne's Bristol Par. Reg.

Stuart. Peyton's Hist. of Augusta Co., Va. Richmond Standard, I. Johnston's Old Va. Clerks. Wm. and Mary Quar., IV, VI. Va. Co. Records, I, II, VI. History of the Stewart, Elliott and Dunwody Families, by J. G. Bulloch, 1895. The First Families of Upper Georgia, by G. R. Gilmer, 1855. Green's Kentucky Families.

Stubblefield. Va. Co. Records, I, III, VI.

Stubbs. Descendants of John Stubbs of Gloucester Co., Va., by Wm. Carter Stubbs, 1902. Wm. and Mary Quar., II.

Sturdevant. Richmond Standard, III. Chamberlayne's Bristol Par. Reg.

Sturman. Wm. and Mary Quar., IV.

Sublett. A History of the Sobletts of Powhatan Co., Va., by S. B. Sublett, 1896.

Suddarth. Woods-McAfee Memorial, by Woods and Durett, 1905. Wood's Hist. of Albemarle Co.

Sullivan. Va. Co. Records, I.

Sullivant. Paxton's Marshall Family. Sullivant Family, by Joseph Sullivant, 1874.

Summers. Middlesex, Va., Par. Reg.

Sumner. Va. Hist. Mag., XI.

Sumter. Wood's Hist. of Albemarle Co.

Sutherland. Va. Co. Records, I, VI. Wood's Hist. of Albemarle.

Sutton. Va. Co. Records, I. Middlesex Par. Reg. Wm. and Mary Quar., VIII, XIX.

Swaine. Goode's Va. Cousins. Va. Co. Records, I.

Swan or Swann. Meade's Old Fam. and Churches. Richmond Standard, III. Va. Co. Records, II, V, VI. Warfield's Anne Arundel and Howard Cos., Md. Wm. and Mary Quar., IV, VI, VIII, XI, XII, XVI. Va. Hist. Mag., III. MSS. Ped. of the Genealogical Assn.

Swearingen. The Swearingen Family, by H. H. Swearingen, 1894. Warfield's Anne Arundel and Howard Cos., Md.

Sweeney. Wm. and Mary Quar., XVI. Va. Co. Records, VI.

Swoope. Saunder's Early Settlers of Alabama, 1899.

Syme. Meade's Old Fam. and Churches. Richmond Standard, II, III. Slaughter's Bristol Par. Slaughter's St. Mark's Par. Wm. and Mary Quar., I, IV, VI, XI.

Symons. Va. Co. Records, VI.

Tabb. Goode's Va. Cousins. Hayden's Va. Gen. Meade's Old Fam. and Churches. Richmond Standard, III. Wm. and Mary Quar., III, IV, VII, XIII, XIV. Va. Co. Records, IV, VI. Lee of Va., by E. J. Lee, 1895.

Taberer. Wm. and Mary Quar., VII.

Taberner. Va. Hist. Mag., VI.

Talbot. Meade's Old Fam. and Churches. Wm. and Mary Quar., IX, X. Va. Hist. Mag., X. Va. Co. Records, I, II, VI. Chamberlayne's Bristol Par. Reg. Warfield's Anne Arundel and Howard Cos., Md. The Thomas Book, by L. B. Thomas. Lower Norfolk Co. Antiquary. Habersham Hist. Coll. of Ga., II. The Descendants of Richard Talbott of Anne Arundel Co., Md., by Ida M. Shirk, 1910. MSS. Ped. of the Genealogical Assn.

Taliaferro. Meade's Old Fam. and Churches. Richmond Standard, II, III, IV. Some Va. Families, by H. L. McIlhany, 1903. Va. Hist. Mag., V. Paxton's Marshall Family. Va. Co. Records, I, II, VI, VII. Goodwyn's Hist. of Bruton Church. Crozier's Hist. of the Buckner Family, 1907. Wm. and Mary Quar., V, VIII, X, XII, XIX. Descendants of Mordecai Cooke of Va., by W. C. Stubbs, 1896. Saunder's Early Settlers of Alabama. Richmond Critic, 16th Nov., 1889.

Talman. Wm. and Mary Quar., III. Va. Co. Records, V. St. Peter's Par. Reg., New Kent, Va.

Tapscott. Wm. and Mary Quar., VI, VIII.

Tarpley. Wm. and Mary Quar., XVIII. Va. Hist. Mag., VII.

Tarrant. Va. Co. Records, V.

Tasker. Maryland Hist. Mag., IV.

Tate. Goode's Va. Cousins. Peyton's Hist. of Augusta Co., Va. Some Va. Families, by H. M. McIlhany, 1903.

Tatem. Chamberlayne's Bristol Par. Reg. Va. Co. Records, VI.

Taverner. Va. Hist. Mag., VII.

Tayloe. Meade's Old Fam. and Churches. Wm. and Mary Quar., VI, VIII, XI. Va. Co. Records, I. Va. Hist. Mag., XVII. The Willis Family of Va., by Byrd C. and Richard H. Willis, 1898.

Taylor. Oliver's Carter Family Tree. Hayden's Va. Gen. Meade's Old Fam. and Churches. Richmond Standard, II, III, IV. Slaughter's St. Mark's Par. Wm. and Mary Quar., III, V, VII, VIII, XI, XII. Va. Hist. Mag., VII, VIII. Richmond Critic, 1890. Richmond Sunday Times, 1898. Robertson Gen., by W. K. Anderson, 1900. Green's Hist. of Culpeper Co., Va. Some Va. Families, by H. L. McIlhany, 1903. Wood's Hist. of Albemarle Co. Va. Co. Records, I, II, V, VI, VII. St. Peter's Par. Reg., New Kent. Middlesex Par. Reg. Goodwyn's Hist. of Bruton Church, Va. Chamberlayne's Bristol Par. Reg. Lower Norfolk Co. Antiquary. Of Sceptred Race, by Annah R. Watson, 1910. Some Notable Families of America, by Annah R. Watson, 1898. First Families of Upper Georgia, by G. R. Gilmer, 1855. Green's Kentucky Families. Paxton's Marshall Family. So. Carolina Hist. and Genl. Mag., VIII.

Tazewell. Meade's Old Fam. and Churches. Richmond Standard, II. Robertson's Pocahontas' Descendants. Wm. and Mary Quar., I. Va. Co. Records, V, VII. Grigsby's Tazewell Gen.

Teackle. Hanson's Hist. of Old Kent, Md.

Tebbs. Paxton's Marshall Family.

Temple. Richmond Standard, IV. Va. Hist. Mag., XII, XVIII. Va. Co. Records, I, II, V. Wm. and Mary Quar., XIII. Chamberlayne's Bristol Par. Reg.

Tennant. Va. Co. Records, I.

Terrell. The Lewis Family, by W. T. Lewis, 1893. Slaughter's St. Mark's Par. Wood's Hist. of Albemarle. Va. Hist. Mag., XVI. Wm. and Mary Quar., XIII. Va. Co. Records, I, VI. Notes on the Terrell Family of Va., by E. H. Terrell, 1907.

Terry. Meade's Old Fam. and Churches. Va. Co. Records, I, VI.

Thacher. Richmond Standard, III. Va. Co. Records, VI.

Thacker. Hayden's Va. Gen. Wm. and Mary Quar., VIII, XV. Va. Co. Record, I, VI. Middlesex Par. Reg.

Theleball. Lower Norfolk Co. Antiquary. Va. Co. Records, VI.

Thilman. Middlesex, Va., Par. Reg.

Thom. Green's Hist. of Culpeper Co., Va.

Thomas. Richmond Standard, III. Slaughter's Hist. of St. Mark's Par. Green's Hist. of Culpeper Co. Gleanings of Va. History, by Wm. F. Boogher. The Thomas Family of Md., by L. B. Thomas, 1877. The Thomas Family, by L. B. Thomas, 1883. The Thomas Book, by L. B. Thomas, 1896. Wood's Hist. of Albemarle. Va. Co. Records, I, II, VI, VII. Middlesex, Va., Par. Reg. St. Peter's Par. Reg., New Kent. Wm. and Mary Quar., VII. Warfield's Anne Arundel and Howard Cos., Md. Hanson's Hist. of Old Kent, Md. Munsell's American Ancestry, VII.

Thompson. Hayden's Va. Gen. Slaughter's St. Mark's Par. Habersham's Hist. Coll. of Ga., I. Va. Hist. Mag., I. Green's Hist. of Culpeper Co., Va. Wood's Hist. of Albemarle. Va. Co. Records, I, II, V, VI, VII. Goodwyn's Hist. of Bruton Church.

Middlesex, Va., Par. Reg. St. Peter's Par. Reg., New Kent. Rootes Fam. of Va., by W. C. Torrence, 1906. Wm. and Mary Quar., XVII. Some Notable Families of America, by Annah R. Watson, 1898.

Thomson. Richmond Standard, III. Va. Co. Records, I, II. Wm. and Mary Quar., III, VII, X. So. Carolina Hist. and Genl. Mag., III.

Thornton. Goode's Va. Cousins. Hayden's Va. Gen. Meade's Old Fam. and Churches. The Meriwethers and Their Connections, by L. H. A. Minor, 1892. Richmond Standard, II, III. Slaughter's St. Mark's Par. Wm. and Mary Quar., II, III, IV, V, VI, VIII, X, XIX. Va. Co. Records, I, II, V, VI, VII. Rootes Fam. of Va., by W. C. Torrence, 1906. Of Sceptred Race, by Annah W. Robinson, 1910. Some Notable Families of America, by Annah R. Watson, 1898. Green's Kentucky Families.

Thoroughgood. Richmond Standard, IV. Va. Hist. Mag., II, III, V. Wm. and Mary Quar., IV. Va. Co. Records, V, VI, VII. Lower Norfolk Co. Antiquary.

Thorp or Thorpe. Meade's Old Fam. and Churches. Goodwyn's Hist. of Bruton Church. Wm. and Mary Quar., III, IX. Va. Hist. Mag., IV, XII. Va. Co. Records, II, V.

Throckmorton. Slaughter's St. Mark's Par. Welle's Washington Gen. Wm. and Mary Quar., II, III, IV, V, XI, XIII, XIV, XIX. Va. Hist. Mag., VI, VIII, IX, X, XI, XII, XIII, XIV, XV. Descendants of Mordecai Cooke of Va., by W. C. Stubbs. Of Sceptred Race, by Annah R. Watson, 1910.

Thruston. Wm. and Mary Quar., III. IV, V, VI, VII, VIII, XIII. Va. Co. Records, I, V, VI. Crozier's Buckners of Va. Descendants of Mordecai Cooke of Va., by W. C. Stubbs, 1896.

Thurman. Wood's Hist. of Albemarle.

Thurston. Va. Co. Records, I.

Thweatt. Richmond Standard, III. Habersham Hist. Coll. of Ga., I. Va. Hist. Mag., VII. Chamberlayne's Bristol Par. Reg.

Tilden. Hanson's Hist. of Old Kent, Md. Maryland Hist. Mag., I.

Tilghman. The Thomas Book, by L. B. Thomas, 1896. Hanson's Hist. of Old Kent, Md. Maryland Hist. Mag., I. Chamberlayne's Bristol Par. Reg. Saunder's Early Settlers of Ala.

Tiernan. The Tiernan Family in Maryland, by C. B. Tiernan, 1898. The Tiernan and Other Families, by C. B. Tiernan, 1901.

Timberlake. Wood's Hist. of Albemarle. Middlesex, Va., Par. Reg.

Timson. Wm. and Mary Quar., II, III, V, XVII. Goodwyn's Hist. of Bruton Church. Va. Co. Records, V.

Tindall. The Gentry Family of Va., by Richard Gentry, 1909.

Tirrey. Va. Co. Records, V.

Todd. Warfield's Hist. of Anne Arundel and Howard Cos., Md. The Edwards and Todd Families, by G. H. Edwards, 1894. Meade's Old Families and Churches. Richmond Standard, III. Slaughter's St. Mark's Par. Va. Hist. Mag., III. Va. Co. Records, I, VI. Wm. and Mary Quar., III.

Toler. Richmond Standard, III. Wm. and Mary Quar., VIII.

Tomlin. Hayden's Va. Gen. Va. Hist. Mag., V. Va. Co. Records, VI.

Tompkies. Wm. and Mary Quar., VIII, XI.

Tompkins. Wm. and Mary Quar., XVI. Wood's Hist. of Albemarle. Va. Co. Records, I.

Took. Wm. and Mary Quar., VII.

Tooker. Va. Co. Records, V.

Tooley. Wood's Hist. of Albemarle.

Torrence. Rootes Fam. of Va., by W. C. Torrence, 1906.

Towles. Cabell's Sketches of Lynchburg. Va. Hist. Mag., VIII, IX. Va. Co. Records, I, V, VI. Middlesex, Va., Par. Register.

Townes. Slaughter's St. Mark's Par. Richmond Standard, III.

Townsend. Munsell's American Ancestry, VII. Va. Hist. Mag., IX, XI. Va. Co. Records, VI.

Townley. Townley Family of New Jersey and Maryland, by F. A. Hill, 1888.

Trabue. Va. His. Collections, V. Va. Hist. Mag., IV.

Tracy. The English Ancestry of Gov. William Tracy of Va., by Dwight Tracy, 1908.

Travers. Hayden's Va. Gen. Meade's Old Fam. and Churches. Richmond Standard, III. Wm. and Mary Quar., IV. Va. Co. Records, VI.

Travis. Meade's Old Fam. and Churches. Richmond Standard, II. Wm. and Mary Quar., I, V, VI, VII, XIV, XVIII. Va. Hist. Mag., VI. Cradle of the Republic, by L. G. Tyler, 1906.

Traylor. Chamberlayne's Bristol Par. Reg.

Trent. Meade's Old Fam. and Churches. Peyton's Hist. of Augusta Co., Va. Va. Co. Records, VI.

Trevilian. Richmond Standard, II.

Trezevant. So. Carolina Hist. and Genl. Mag., III. Richmond Standard, II.

Trigg. Va. Co. Records, I. Middlesex, Va., Par. Reg.

Trimble. Old King William Homes and Families, by P. N. Clarke, 1897. Va. Co. Records, II.

Triplett. Wm. and Mary Quar., X. Va. Co. Records, I.

Trotter. Habersham Hist. Coll. of Ga., II.

Trout. Some Va. Families, by H. M. McIlhany, 1903.

True. Va. Co. Records, I.

Trussell. Va. Hist. Mag., IV.

Tuck. Richmond Standard, III.

Tucker. Bolling Gen., by Robert Bolling, 1868. Goode's Va. Cousins. Cabell's Sketches of Lynchburg. Meade's Old Fam. and Churches. Slaughter's Bristol Par. Welle's Washington Genealogy. Wm and Mary Quar., I, II, IV, V, VI, VIII, X, XII. Goodwyn's Hist. of Bruton Church. Va. Co. Records, III, V, VI, VII. Va. Hist. Mag., I, IV, IX, XVII. St. Peter's Par. Reg., New Kent. Chamberlayne's Bristol Par. Reg. Lower Norfolk Co. Antiquary. Richmond, Va., Critic, 1889. The Tucker Family of Bermuda, by Thos. A. Emmett, 1898.

Tulladgh. Wm. and Mary Quar., VII.

Tulley. Richmond Standard, III.

Tunstall. Va. Hist. Mag., XIV. Va. Co. Records, II, VI.

Turberville. Meade's Old Fam. and Churches. Wm. and Mary Quar., IV, V, VII. Va. Co. Records, V. Lee of Va., by E. J. Lee, 1895.

Tureman. Va. Co. Records, I.

Turnbull. Johnston's Old Va. Clerks.

Turner. Meade's Old Fam. and Churches. Richmond Standard, III. Slaughter's St. Mark's Par. Wm. and Mary Quar., I, IX, XI. Wood's Hist. of Albemarle. Va. Co. Records, I, II, V, VI, VII. Goodwyn's Hist. of Bruton Church. St. Peter's Par. Reg., New Kent, Va. Chamberlayne's Bristol Par. Bulloch and Allied Families, by J. G. Bulloch, 1892. MSS. Ped. of the Genealogical Assn.

Turnley. Va. Co. Records, I.

Turpin. MSS. Coll. at the Va. Hist. Society. Va. Co. Records, VI.

Tutt. Va. Co. Records, I, II.

Twyman. Wood's Hist. of Albemarle. Va. Co. Records, I.

Tyler. Campbell's Hist. of Va. Goode's Va. Cousins. Meade's Old Fam. and Churches. Richmond, Va., Critic, 1888. Richmond Standard, I. Wm. and Mary Quar., I, II, III, IV, VI, XII, XVI, XVII. Va. Co. Records, I. Goodwyn's Hist. of Bruton Church. Letters and Times of the Tylers, by L. G. Tyler, 1897. The Tylers of Mass., Conn., R. I., Va., Md., and N. J., by W. Tyler Brigham.

Tyson. The Thomas Book, by L. B. Thomas, 1896.

Underhill. Wm. and Mary Quar., II. Va. Co. Records, II, V, VI.

Underwood. Wm. and Mary Quar., VII, X, XIV. MSS. Coll. on Underwood Fam. at the Va. Historical Society. Va. Hist. Mag., III. Middlesex Par. Reg. Va. Co. Records, II, VI.

Upshaw. Meade's Old Fam. and Churches.

Upshur. Wm. and Mary Quar., III, VII.

Upton. Wm. and Mary Quar., VI, VII. Va. Hist. Mag., III, VI. Va. Co. Records, VI.

Urquhart. Goode's Va. Cousins. Saunder's Early Settlers of Ala.

Utie. Wm. and Mary Quar., IV.

Valentine. Slaughter's St. Mark's Par. Va. Hist. Mag., VI. Wm. and Mary Quar., III, VII.

Vance. Hayden's Va. Gen. Va. Co. Records, II.

Van Meter. The Van Meter Family of Va. and Ky., by B. F. Van Meter, 1901. The Van Metre and Other Families, by S. G. Smyth, 1909.

Van Zandt. Richmond Standard, III.

Vass. Va. Co. Records, I.

Vasser. Wm. and Mary Quar., VII. Va. Hist. Mag., VI.

Vaughan. Goode's Va. Cousins. Meade's Old Fam. and Churches. Va. Co. Records, I, III, VI. St. Peter's Par. Reg., New Kent. Chamberlayne's Bristol Par. Reg.

Vaulx. Wm. and Mary Quar., II, III, IV, XIV.

Vause. Middlesex Par. Reg.

Vawter. The Vawter Family in America, by Grace V. Bicknell, 1905.

Veale. Va. Co. Records, VI.

Veazey. Warfield's Anne Arundel and Howard Cos., Md. Hanson's Old Kent, Md.

Venable. Goode's Va. Cousins. Meade's Old Fam. and Churches. Richmond Standard, III. Wm. and Mary Quar., XV. Va. Hist. Mag., VII.

Vernon. Wm. and Mary Quar., V.

Vicars. Va. Co. Records, VI.

Vickers. Wm. and Mary Quar., VII. Hanson's Old Kent, Md.

Villain. Va. Hist. Collections, V.

Vines. Wm. and Mary Quar., VIII.

Vivian. Hayden's Va. Gen. Middlesex Par. Reg. Wm. and Mary Quar., XV.

Wade. Meade's Old Churches and Fam. St. Peter's Par. Reg., New Kent. Wm. and Mary Quar., I. Va. Co. Records, VI.

Waddell. Johnston's Old Va. Clerks. Wood's Hist. of Albemarle. Peyton's Hist. of Augusta Co., Va. St. Peter's Par. Reg., New Kent.

Waddey. Va. Co. Records, II, III. St. Peter's Par. Reg., New Kent.

Waggaman. Wm. and Mary Quar., II, XVII.

Waggener or Waggenor. Richmond Standard, III. Va. Co. Records, I, II. Slaughter's Hist. of Truro Par., Va., 1908.

Wakefield. Va. Co. Records, VI.

Waldoe. Va. Co. Records, V.

Waldruf. Richmond Standard, II.

Walke. Richmond Standard, III. Robertson's Pocahontas' Descendants. Wm. and Mary Quar., II. Va. Hist. Mag., V. Va. Co. Records, III, V. Lower Norfolk Co. Antiquary.

Walker. Goode's Va. Cousins. Meade's Old Fam. and Churches. Richmond Standard, II, III, IV. Robertson's Pocahontas' Descendants. Slaughter's Bristol Par. Slaughter's Fry Gen. Slaughter's St. Mark's Par. Wm. and Mary Quar., IV, V, VI, VIII, IX, X, XIII, XIV, XVI, XVIII. Va. Hist. Mag., I, IV, VII, X. John Walker of Wigton, Scotland and of Va., by Emma S. White, 1902. Wood's Hist. of Albemarle Co. Va. Co. Records, I, II, III, IV, VI, VII. Middlesex, Va., Par. Reg. St. Peter's Par. Reg., New Kent. Chamberlayne's Bristol Par. Reg. Of Sceptred Race, by Annah R. Watson. Some Notable Families of America, by Annah R. Watson. The Thomas Family of Md., by L. B. Thomas. Jones Gen., by L. H. Jones, 1891. The Walkers of Toaping Castle, Md., by S. H. Walker, 1883.

Wall. Chamberlayne's Bristol Par. Reg.

Wallace. Hayden's Va. Gen. Slaughter's St. Mark's Par. Wm. and Mary Quar., IV, VIII, IX, X, XIII. Va. Hist. Mag.. VIII. Wood's Hist. of Albemarle. Va. Co. Records, I, II, V, VI.

Waller. Bolling Gen., by Robert Bolling, 1868. Hayden's Va. Gen. Meade's Old Fam. and Churches. Richmond Standard, II, III. Johnston's Old Va. Clerks. Wm. and Mary Quar., IV, VIII, IX, X, XIII. Va. Co. Records, I, II, V, VI. Richmond Critic, 5th

April, 1900. Middlesex Par. Reg. Goodwyn's Hist. of Bruton
Church. Old King William Homes and Families, by P. N. Clarke,
1897.

Walthall. Chamberlayne's Bristol Par. Reg. Saunder's Early Settlers of Alabama. Va. Co. Records, VI.

Walton. Meade's Old Va. Fam. and Churches. Richmond Standard,
I, II, III Va. Hist. Mag., I, XI. Wm. and Mary Quar., XV.
St. Peter's Par. Reg., New Kent. Habersham Hist. Coll. of Ga.,
I, II. Va. Co. Records, VI, VII. The Waltons of Va., by Mrs.
W. C. Stubbs, in Gulf State Hist. Mag., Vol. II, 1903. Saunder's
Early Settlers of Alabama. MSS. Ped. of the Genealogical Assn.

Ward. Meade's Old Fam. and Churches. Robertson's Pocahontas' Descendants. Va. Hist. Mag., II. Va. Co. Records, I, II, VI.
Lower Norfolk Co. Antiquary.

Warden. The Warden Family, by Wm. A. Warden, 1901.

Ware. Hayden's Va. Gen. Meade's Old Fam. and Churches. Richmond Standard, III. Va. Co. Records, I, VI. Middlesex Par.
Reg. Wm. and Mary Quar., V.

Warfield. Warfield's Anne Arundel and Howard Cos., Md. The
Thomas Book, by L. B. Thomas.

Waring. Va. Hist. Mag., V, XI. The Bowies and Their Kin, by W.
W. Bowie. Jones Gen., by L. H. Jones, 1891.

Warner. Richmond Standard, III, IV. Va. Hist. Mag., II. A Royal
Lineage, by Annah R. Watson, 1901. Wm. and Mary Quar., II,
IX, XV. Va. Co. Records, V, VI. Of Sceptred Race, by Annah
R. Watson, 1910. Gren's Kentucky Families.

Warren. Richmond Standard, II. Va. Hist. Mag., VI. Va. Co.
Records, I, II, V, VI, VII. St. Peter's Par. Reg., New Kent.

Warwick. Cabell's Sketches of Lynchburg. Middlesex, Va., Par.
Reg.

Washington. Sparks' Life of Washington, 1847. Southern Bivouac,
1886. Wm. and Mary Quar., I, II, III, IV, V, VI, VIII, X, XIII,
XV. Va. Co. Records, I, II, IV, V, VI, VII. Middlesex Par.
Reg. Goodwyn's Hist. of Bruton Church. Crozier's Hist. of the
Buckners of Va. Habersham Hist. Coll. of Ga., I. Lee of Va.,
by E. J. Lee. Green's Kentucky Families. Paxton's Marshall Fam-
ily. Descendants of John Washington of Va., in Heraldic Jour-
nal, II, 1866. Ancestry of George Washington in the Athenæum,
London, 19th Oct., 1899. The English Home of the Washingtons,
in Harper's Monthly Mag., March, 1879. Welle's History of the
Washington Family, 1879. The Washington Family, by Albert
Welles, 1881. The English Ancestry of George Washington, by
H. F. Waters, 1889. The Washington Family in America, by
Thornton A. Washington, 1891. Wills of the Washington Family,
by W. C. Ford, 1891. Neill's Life of Washington, 1892. The
Washington Family, by W. C. Ford, 1893. The Irish Washing-
tons, by Geo. Washington and Thos. H. Murray, 1898. Washing-
ton Gen. in N. Y. Genl. and Biog. Record, Vol. XXXIII. Wash-
ington and Mount Vernon, by M. D. Conway, 1889. Washington
Wills, by Joseph M. Toner, 1891. Bolling Gen. Campbell's Hist.
of Va. Hayden's Va. Gen. Meade's Old Fam. and Churches. The
Page Family, by R. C. M. Page, 1883. Richmond Standard, III.
Slaughter's St. Mark's Par.

Waters. Habersham Hist. Coll. of Ga., I. Va. Hist. Mag., I, II, IX, XI. Wm. and Mary Quar., VI. Va. Co. Records, V, VI. MSS. Ped. of the Genealogical Assn.

Watkins. Meade's Old Fam. and Churches. Richmond Standard, II, III. Va. Hist. Mag., IX. Moore's Hist. of Henrico Par., Va. Va. Co. Records, I, II, VI, VII. Va. Hist. Collections, V. Wm. and Mary Quar., IX. Warfield's Anne Arundel and Howard Cos., Md. Saunder's Early Settlers of Alabama. Thos. Watkins of Chickahominy, Va., by F. N. Watkins, 1852.

Watson. Meade's Old Fam. and Churches. Va. Hist. Mag., VI. Wood's Hist. of Albemarle. St. Peter's Par. Reg., New Kent. Of Sceptred Race, by Annah R. Watson, 1910. Va. Co. Records, VI, VII.

Watts. Wood's Hist. of Albemarle. Va. Co. Records, I, II, VI, VII. Middlesex Par. Reg.

Waugh. Wm. and Mary Quar., XV, XVII.

Wayles. Wm. and Mary Quar., II, VI.

Wayne. Richmond Standard, I.

Wayt. Peyton's Hist. of Augusta Co., Va. Wood's Hist. of Albemarle.

Weaver. St. Peter's Par. Reg., New Kent. Va. Co. Records, IV, VI.

Webb. Hayden's Va. Gen. Va. Hist. Mag., III, VII. Wm. and Mary Quar., V, VII. Va. Co. Records, I, III, V, VI, VII. Middlesex Par. Reg. St. Peter's Par. Reg., New Kent. Saunder's Early Settlers of Alabama.

Webster. Meade's Old Fam. and Churches. St. Peter's Par. Reg., New Kent. Va. Co. Records, VI, VII.

Weedon. Early Settlers in Alabama, by J. E. Saunders. Va. Co. Records, II, VI, VII.

Wedderburn. Rootes of Va., by W. C. Torrence, 1906.

Weekes. Va. Hist Mag., V. Middlesex Par. Reg.

Weems. Hayden's Va. Gen. Richmond Standard, III.

Weir. Richmond Standard, III. Va. Mag., V. Va. Co. Records, I.

Welch. Va. Co. Records, II, VI, VII.

Weldon. Wm. and Mary Quar., I, VI.

Wellford. Richmond Standard, II. Wm. and Mary Quar., X, XI. Paxton's Marshall Family.

Wells. Goodwyn's Hist. of Bruton Church. Chamberlayne's Bristol Par. Reg. Va. Co. Records, VI.

Welmoth. Wm. and Mary Quar., VII.

Welsh. Warfield's Anne Arundel and Howard Cos., Md. Va. Co. Records, I.

Wertenbaker. Wood's Hist of Albemarle.

West. Goode's Va. Cousin. Meade's Old Fam. and Churches. Neill's Va. Carolorum. Richmond Standard, I, II, III. Southern Bivouac. 1886. Wm. and Mary Quar., II, III, V, VII, VIII, X, XVI. Va. Hist. Mag., I, II, VIII. Va. Co. Records, I, II, V, VI, VII. Lower Norfolk Co. Antiquary. Chamberlayne's Bristol Par. Of Sceptred Race, by Annah R. Watson. Richmond Critic, 17th Feb, 1889. Munsell's American Ancestry. VII.

Weston. Middlesex, Va., Par. Reg.

Westwood. Meade's Old Fam. and Churches. Wm. and Mary Quar., IX. Va. Co. Records, V.

Wethered. The Thomas Book, by L. B. Thomas. Hanson's Old Kent, Md.

Whaley. Wm. and Mary Quar., I, IV. Goodwyn's Hist. of Bruton Church. The Whaley Family, by Rev. S. Whaley, 1901.

Wharton. Va. Co. Records, I. Goodwyn's Hist. of Bruton Church.

Wheeler. Wood's Hist. of Albemarle. Va. Co. Records, I, VI, VII. Middlesex Par. Reg.

Whitaker. Richmond Standard, III. Va. Hist. Mag., XI. Middlesex Par. Reg.

White. White Family of Maryland, by W. W. Bronson, 1879. Richmond Standard, III. Va. Hist. Mag., IX, XI. Wm. and Mary Quar., II, VI, VII, VIII. Wood's Hist. of Albemarle. Va. Co. Records, I, II, VI, VII. Goodwyn's Hist. of Bruton Church. Lower Norfolk Co. Antiquary. Saunder's Early Settlers of Alabama. Ancestry of the Children of James W. White, by W. F. Cregar, 1888.

Whitehead. Wm. and Mary Quar., XI. Va. Co. Records, V. Lower Norfolk Co., Antiquary.

Whitehill. Goode's Va. Cousins.

Whitehurst. Lower Norfolk Co. Antiquary.

Whitesides. Some Va. Families, by H. L. McIlhany, 1903.

Whiting. Hayden's Va. Gen. Meade's Old Fam. and Churches. Welles' Washington Gen. Va. Co. Records, I, V. Wm. and Mary Quar., VIII. Descendants of Mordecai Cooke of Va., by W. C. Stubbs, 1896. Blair, Banister and Braxton Families, by F. Horner, 1898. Va. Hist. Mag., XVIII. Memoir of the Rev. Samuel Whiting and His Wife, Elizabeth St. John, by Wm. Whiting, 1873.

Whitlock. St. Peter's Par. Reg., New Kent.

Whittle. Robertson's Pocahontas' Descendants. Slaughter's Bristol Par. Richmond, Va., Critic, 4th Aug., 1889.

Wiatt. Cabell's Lynchburg Sketches. Wm. and Mary Quar., III, X, XII. Va. Co. Records, I.

Wickes. Hanson's Hist. of Old Kent, Md.

Wickham. Oliver's Carter Tree. Meade's Old Fam. and Churches. Richmond Standard, IV.

Wickliffe. Wm. and Mary Quar., X, XV.

Wilcox. Meade's Old Fam. and Churches. Va. Hist. Mag., II.

Wild. Wm. and Mary Quar., IV.

Wilkerson. Goode's Va. Cousins. Va. Co. Records, I.

Wilkins. Meade's Old Fam. and Churches. Lower Norfolk Co. Antiquary. Middlesex Par. Reg. Va. Co. Records, VI, VII.

Wilkinson. Wood's Hist. of Albemarle. Va. Co. Records, I, III, VI. Goodwyn's Hist. of Bruton Church. St. Peter's Par. Reg., New Kent. Wm. and Mary Quar., VIII.

Willcox. Wm. and Mary Quar., XI, XVI.

Williams. Meade's Old Fam. and Churches. Richmond Standard,
III. Slaughter's Hist. of St. Mark's Par. Johnston's Old Va.
Clerks. Va. Hist. Mag., X. Green's Hist. of Culpeper Co. Va.
Co. Records, I, II, VI, VII. Middlesex Par. Reg. St. Peter's
Par. Reg., New Kent. Wm. and Mary Quar., V. Goodwyn's
Hist. of Bruton Church. Lower Norfolk Co. Antiquary. Cham-
berlayne's Hist. of Bristol Par. Eminent North Carolinians, by
J. W. Wheeler. Hist. of No. Carolina, by J. H. Wheeler. The
Alstons of No. and So. Carolina, by J. A. Groves, 1902.

Williamson. Richmond Standard, III, IV. Wm. and Mary Quar.,
VII, IX, XII. Va. Hist. Mag., V, VI. Va. Co. Records, I, VI.
Lower Norfolk Co. Antiquary. Middlesex Par. Reg. Wheeler's
Hist. of No. Carolina.

Willis. Meade's Old Fam. and Churches. Richmond Standard, III.
Slaughter's Fry Gen. Wm. and Mary Quar., III, V, VI. Va.
Hist. Mag., V, X. Willis Family of Va., by Byrd C., and Richard
H. Willis, 1898. Va. Co. Records, I, V, VI, VII. Middlesex Par.
Reg. St. Peter's Par. Reg., New Kent. MSS. Ped. of the Genea-
logical Assn.

Willoughby. Neill's Va. Carolorum. Va. Hist. Mag., I, IV. Va. Co.
Records, I, V, VI, VII. Lower Norfolk Co. Antiquary. Of
Sceptred Race, by Annah R. Watson. Some Notable Families of
America, by Annah R. Watson.

Wills. Richmond Standard, III. Va. Co. Records, III, VI, VII. Wm.
and Mary Quar., VII.

Wilmer. Slaughter's Bristol Par. Hanson's Old Kent, Md.

Wilson. Johnston's Old Va. Clerks. Va. Co. Records, I, II, III, V,
VI, VII. Va. Hist. Coll., V. Wm. and Mary Quar., VII, IX.
Chamberlayne's Bristol Par. Reg. Lower Norfolk Co. Antiquary.
Hanson's Old Kent, Md.

Winder. Warfield's Anne Arundel and Howard Cos., Md.

Winfree. Winfree of Va., by Mrs. W. C. Stubbs, in Gulf States Hist.
Mag., II, 1903. St. Peter's Par. Reg., New Kent, Va.

Wingate. Va. Hist. Mag., XV.

Wingfield. Goode's Va. Cousins. Wood's Hist. of Albemarle. Chamberlayne's Bristol Par. Reg.

Winn. Va. Hist. Mag., VI. Wood's Hist. of Albemarle. Middlesex
Par. Reg. Va. Co. Records, VI.

Winslow. Va. Hist. Mag., III. Va. Co. Records, I.

Winston. Hayden's Va. Gen. Cabell's Lynchburg Sketches. Meade's
Old Fam. and Churches. Richmond Standard, I, II. Slaughter's
St. Mark's Par. Winston Fam., A MSS. Ped. of the Va. Hist.
Society. Va. Hist. Mag., V. Green's Hist. of Culpeper Co.
Moore's Hist. of Henrico Par. Va. Co. Records, I. Isaac Win-
ston and His Descendants, by Elizabeth W. C. Hendrick, 1899.
Va. Hist. Collections, V.

Wise. Meade's Old Fam. and Churches. Richmond Critic, 1888.
Johnston's Old Va. Clerks. Richmond Standard, IV. Va. Co.
Records, V, VI, VII.

Wishart. Lower Norfolk Co. Antiquary.

Witham. Wm. and Mary Quar., II. Va. Co. Records, V.

Wither. Va. Hist. Mag., XV.

Withers. Meade's Old Fam. and Churches. Richmond Standard, II, III. Slaughter's Bristol Par. Va. Hist. Mag., VI, VII. Wm. and Mary Quar., XIII. Va. Co. Records, V, VI, VII. Saunder's Early Settlers of Alabama.

Witherspoon. Nathaniel Evans of So. Carolina, by J. D. Evans.

Withrow. Richmond Standard, III.

Womack. Va. Co. Records, VI.

Wood. Hayden's Va. Gen. Meade's Old Fam. and Churches. Minor's Meriwether Gen. Richmond Standard, II, III. Johnston's Old Va. Clerks. Va. Hist. Mag., III, V. Wm. and Mary Quar., VI, VII, X, XII. Wood's Hist. of Albemarle. Va. Co. Records, I, II, VI, VII. Middlesex Par. Reg. St. Peter's Par. Reg., New Kent. Wood Family of Va., by M. B. Wood, 1893.

Woodfolk. Va. Co. Records, I.

Woodford. Richmond Standard, III. Va. Hist. Mag., V. Va. Co. Records, I, V. Jones Gen., by L. H. Jones, 1891.

Woodhouse. Va. Hist. Mag., VI, VIII. Wm. and Mary Quar., I, II, V, XII. Va. Co. Records, V. Lower Norfolk Co. Antiquary.

Woodley. Wm. and Mary Quar., VII.

Woodlief. Va. Hist. Mag., II.

Woodroof. Va. Co. Records, I.

Woodrop. Va. Co. Records, III. Wm. and Mary Quar., XI.

Woods. The Woods-McAfee Memorial, Containing an Account of John Woods and James McAfee of Ireland, and Their Descendants in America, by Rev. Neander M. Woods and Reuben T. Durett, 1905. Richmond Standard, III. Wood's Hist. of Albemarle. Va. Co. Records, II.

Woodson. Meade's Old Fam. and Churches. Richmond Standard, II. Wm. and Mary Quar., VII, IX, X, XI, XVI. Wood's Hist. of Albemarle. Va. Co. Records, VI, VII. Green's Kentucky Families.

Woodville. Meade's Old Fam. and Churches. Slaughter's St. Mark's Par. Green's Hist. of Culpeper.

Woodward. Warfield's Anne Arundel and Howard Cos., Md. So. Carolina Hist. and Genl. Mag., VIII. Va. Hist. Mag., V. Wm. and Mary Quar., VII. Va. Co. Records, II, VI, VII.

Woolfolk. Paxton's Marshall Family. Wm. and Mary Quar., XI. Va. Co. Records, I.

Wooton or Wotton. Habersham Hist. Coll. of Ga., II. Wm. and Mary Quar., VII. MSS. Ped. of the Genealogical Assn.

Wormeley. Oliver's Carter Family Tree. De Bows' Review, XXVI. Hayden's Va. Gen. Meade's Old Fam. and Churches. Page Gen., by R. C. M. Page. Southern Bivouac, 1886. Va. Hist. Mag., I, VII, VIII, IX, XVI. Wm. and Mary Quar., III, VI, X. Va. Co. Records, V, VI. Middlesex, Va., Par. Reg.

Worsham. Slaughter's Bristol Par. Chamberlayne's Bristol Par. Reg. Va. Hist. Mag., IX.

Wortham. Va. Hist. Mag., VIII. Middlesex, Va., Par. Reg.

Worthington. Warfield's Anne Arundel and Howard Cos., Md. Munsell's American Ancestry, VII. The Bowies and Their Kin, by W. W. Bowie. The Worthington and Plaskitt Families, with Others of Maryland, by Joshua Plaskitt, 1886.

Wray. Va. Hist. Mag., X. Goodwyn's Hist. of Bruton Church. Wm. and Mary Quar., XVIII. Va. Co. Records, V.

Wright. The Wrights of Maryland, by Capt. C. W. Wright, 1907. Warfield's Anne Arundel and Howard Cos., Md. Va. Co. Records, I, II, VI. Middlesex Par. Reg. Wm. and Mary Quar., VIII, XVII. Lower Norfolk Co. Antiquary. Goodwyn's Bruton Church.

Wyatt. Meade's Old Fam. and Churches. Neill's Va. Carolorum. Richmond Standard, II. Wm. and Mary Quar., II, III, VI, X, XII, XVII. Va. Hist. Mag., III, V, VII. Va. Co. Records, I, V. Goodwyn's Bruton Church. St. Peter's Par. Reg., New Kent. Chamberlayne's Bristol Parish. The Gentry Family, by Richard Gentry, 1909. Saunder's Early Settlers of Alabama.

Wyche. Wm. and Mary Quar., XIII, XIV, XV. Va. Co. Records, V.

Wylly. Hist. of the Bulloch Family, by J. G. Bulloch, 1892.

Wynne. Va. Hist. Mag., VI, XI, XIV. Chamberlayne's Bristol Par. Reg. Habersham Hist. Coll. of Ga., II. Va. Co. Records, VI.

Wythe. Campbell's Hist. of Va. Meade's Old Fam. and Churches. Wm. and Mary Quar., II, X, XII, XIII. Goodwyn's Bruton Church.

Yancey. Peyton's Hist. of Augusta Co. Green's Hist. of Culpeper. Wood's Hist. of Albemarle. Wm. and Mary Quar., XVII, X. Va. Co. Records, I. Wheeler's Hist. of No. Carolina.

Yarbrough. Middlesex, Va., Par. Reg.

Yardley. Wm. and Mary Quar., IV.

Yarrington. Middlesex, Va., Par. Reg.

Yates. Hayden's Va. Gen. Meade's Old Fam. and Churches. Richmond Standard, II. Robertson's Pocahontas' Descendants. Va. Hist. Mag., VII. Va. Co. Records, I, VI, VII. Middlesex Par. Reg. Goodwyn's Bruton Church. Wm. and Mary Quar., I, II, III, IV. Saunder's Early Settlers of Ala. Memorials of the Yates Family in England and Va., by A. E. Terrill, 1877.

Yeamans. Wm. and Mary Quar., IV, VI.

Yeardley. Sir George Yeardley, Gov.-General of Va., and Some of Their Descendants, by T. T. Upshur, 1896. Neill's Va. Carolorum. Va. Hist. Mag., I. Va. Co. Records, V.

Yeatman. Wm. and Mary Quar., XIII.

Yelverton. Meade's Old Fam. and Churches.

Yeo. Wm. and Mary Quar., V, IX. Va. Hist. Mag., VII.

Yergain. Wood's Hist. of Albemarle Co.

Yonge. Va. Hist. Mag., XV.

Yowell. Wm. and Mary Quar., IV. St. Peter's Par. Reg., New Kent.

Young. Johnston's Old Va. Clerks. Va. Co. Records, I, II, VI, VII. Wm. and Mary Quar., VII. Saunder's Early Settlers of Alabama. Family Tree of Michael Cadet Young of Brunswick Co., Va., Compiled by C. D. Cowles, 1895.

Yuille. Goodwyn's Hist. of Bruton Church. Va. Co. Records, V.

Zouch. Va. Hist. Mag., XII. Va. Co. Records, V.

ADDENDA

Allen.   The Allens of Lunenburg, Va., by Capt. C. T.
              Allen, 1895.

Beckwith.   Chamberlayne's Bristol Par. Reg. Va.

Hardaway.   The Allens of Lunenburg, Va., by Capt. C. T.
              Allen, 1895.

Langley.   Wm. and Mary Quar. XIX.

Ludwell.   Wm. and Mary Quar. XIX.

Miller.   Alexander Miller of Virginia, and some of his
              descendants by Milo Custer, 1910.

Snead.   The Sneads of Fluvanna, Va., by Mrs. W. E.
              Hatcher, 1910.

Thornton.   Crozier's History of the Buckners of Va., 1907.

www.ingramcontent.com/pod-product-compliance
Lightning Source LLC
Chambersburg PA
CBHW052104270326
41931CB00012B/2881